All inquiries should be addressed to:
Easy Money Press
P.O. Box 50755
Irvine, CA 92619.

ISBN 0-9654563-2-3

Manufactured in the United States of America

Tontine

by

H. C. Wolford

Easy Money Press

DEDICATION

To Sheri,
who helped me with
the sexy parts.

To the others,
who helped me with
the murderous parts.

You know who you were!

Prologue

In times of war, groups of men do horribly immoral acts in the name of God and country, wrapped in the comforting guise of patriotism, and move on, never looking back on the carnage they have produced.

In times of peace, mobs of angry riotous men destroy public property, under a bannered cause, hiding behind a shield, labeled social injustice.

In times of war, individuals filled with rage, commit acts of cruelty unleashed upon their fellow man, released in a blinding burst of violence which in the aftermath is proclaimed valor.

In times of peace, one man's instant of uncontrolled passion takes an unsuspecting life, regretted in the same instant, repented within the label of murder.

In times of war, insane acts make perfect sense, and logic is a luxury afforded little place to flourish. In hindsight, the decision made in the heat of battle by ten best intentioned young men, can make no sense at all.

Thus it was with the 3rd platoon, 7th infantry, U.S. Army, on January 3rd, 1945. On a cold, damp afternoon in France, ten young men came to a much debated decision. It was a decision which made absolute sense at the time, for the times. It was a decision which could come back to destroy them.

Chapter 1

"Hey Sarge," whined Tinker, "do we really have to go anywhere today? It's too damned cold."

Sergeant Cummings did not change his expression in the least. He simply continued polishing yesterday's dirt from his forty-five automatic. When it was sufficiently clean, he holstered it. Pausing to look up into the gray sky, he reached into one of the pockets on his coat and pulled out a pack of cigarettes.

Cupping his hands around the trusted Zippo lighter, Sarge lit a cigarette, drawing a deep drag of the tobacco smoke into his lungs. He exhaled in a long, smoky sigh, clicking his Zippo closed. Pulling the cigarette from his lips, he said, "What's the matter Private Lewis? You got something better to do?"

Realizing it was much too early in the day to get his sergeant upset with him, Tinker reconsidered his original request and replied, "No Sarge. It ain't anything like that at all. I was just thinking about the other guys, that's all."

Private Carter joined the discussion with, “No offense, Tinker, but the thought of you thinking about me, well, you all know what I mean.” The rest of the squad broke out in laughter.

Private Bradley Lewis earned the nickname of Tinker, in part for his habit, or gift, of taking things apart and putting them back together. It was also a conveniently shortened form of Tinkerbell, Peter Pan's fairy companion.

“Hey, Tinker was just trying to get us a day off,” pled Private Johnson, trying to defend Lewis.

Carter could hardly contain his laughter, forcing out, “Red, you are so stupid sometimes. You have no idea what I'm talking about. What did they teach you back in Iowa?”

“Hey, they teached me real good.”

Carter couldn't resist continuing the ribbing. “Does anyone know what the letters in Iowa stand for? I Owe the World an Apology is what I heard.”

Red tried to knock the smile off Carter's face, by throwing a chunk of crusty bread at his chest. “Don't be picking on my state like that, unless you're willing to back it up...”

“Knock it off, all of you,” growled Sgt. Cummings. “Each one of you knuckle-heads has enough bullshit to fill a three-story outhouse, so cram it. Get your gear in order. We're moving out in ten minutes.”

To emphasize his point, Sarge threw his cigarette to the ground and stomped it out with his boot. He pulled the collar up on his coat, grabbed his Thompson sub-machine gun, and huffed off into the bushes to urinate.

Tinker went back to his morning business. When Corporal Bambridge walked by, Tinker said, “Hey, Professor. I hear we're getting some new blood today. Is it true?”

“Yeah it's true. Some new guy, fresh in from home.”

Tinker asked, "When is he getting in?"

The corporal squinted into the brightening sky as if searching for some divine response. Moving his neck around, trying to relieve a cramp, he rubbed his face and said, "Don't really know for sure. I think he's supposed to meet up with us in town this afternoon."

Letting curiosity get the best of him, Tinker asked, "You know where he's from or what's his name?"

A bit perturbed, the corporal said, "For what it's worth, his name is Ross and I think I heard he's from Oklahoma. Now if you don't mind, private, I think you'd better be getting your gear stowed away, before we all decide to leave your sorry ass behind."

Tinker started to say something and then thinking better, decided to let it pass and get on with packing his possessions.

A few minutes later, an obviously relieved sergeant returned from the bushes, verified his gear was ready to move, then got the men's attention with, "Okay ladies. Listen up. You all know the routine. We're heading into town. I know it's hard to focus, but you've got to stay sharp. I don't want to be losing anybody because you really are stupider than you look. Let's get in and get out. Not that you guys should need any incentive, but I've got a surprise for you. I managed to get us a couple of extra days stand down, so when we finish today, we've got four days off."

The squad collectively cheered and thanked Sarge, along with any convenient gods they worshipped. Sarge cut them off in mid-cheer with, "Stow it! We've got a job to do and I'm not going to stand for anyone getting sloppy. Keep your mind on your work or the deal is off. Got it?" Sarge looked around to see if anyone missed his message. "Good. Now get your gear and move out."

Slowly the platoon pulled on their backpacks, slung their weapons over their shoulders, and started trudging up the road into town. Many of the recently liberated towns in this part of France were heavily damaged from gunfire and bombs, and there was no convenient place to house the soldiers. The Army felt it better to leave what was left of the towns and villages, to the residents, so they created camps in the countryside.

Sometimes the towns were within walking distance, but most of the time the men would climb aboard transports for the trip. At times it was almost comical to see. Individual platoons or companies would bivouac in various camouflaged locations in the hillsides. At a predetermined time, they would begin to emerge from their nesting areas and begin to filter down to the staging sites. If this were the city, instead of the French countryside, it would look like residents exiting their buildings and homes, making their way to the corner bus stop.

Sergeant Cummings' men reached the staging area and found their designated transport. One by one, they climbed up, over the lowered tailgate, and took a seat on the bench attached to each side of the transport's cargo area. Finally, all eight men and their gear found a place to sit. Sarge lifted the tailgate into position and latched it closed. He reached up with his right hand, and putting his right foot onto the rear bumper, pulled himself up on the driver's side of the transport.

Sarge banged on the side of the truck with his left hand to get the driver's attention. Waving to the driver like a railroad conductor, Sarge yelled, “All aboard.” With practiced ease, he used the momentum of the truck lurching into gear, to swing his body over the tailgate and into the transport. Setting his equipment on the floor, he said, “I hope you girls all went to the bathroom before we left home.”

Chapter 2

Private Casey Ross was standing near the intersection of two roads when he heard the faint sounds of an approaching truck. As the transport approached, it became possible for him to read the identification numbers on the front bumper. Casey pulled his temporary orders from his pocket and double checked his information. Seeing the numbers matched, he held out his right hand, thumb sticking heavenward, begging for a ride.

The truck slowed and stopped beside the lone figure. The driver leaned out the window and said, "What can I do you for?"

"Muh, name's Ross, sir. I'm supposed to stand here until your truck come along. I'm supposed to meet muh new sergeant, Sergeant Cummings. Do you know where I kin find him?"

The driver lifted his duty cap, and with a handkerchief, he wiped some sweat from his brow and some dirt from his face. "I ain't no sir, tenderfoot. I'm a working stiff just like you. Your sergeant's in the back of the truck."

Private Ross nodded to the driver and shuffled to the rear of the transport. The truck had been driving east, so the morning sun was shining from directly above the canvas covering the cargo area. Looking up into the truck, Casey had to raise his hand to his eyebrows to block the sun. Once his eyes adjusted a bit, he was able to see the stripes on Sarge's sleeve. "Private Ross, reporting as ordered."

Sarge looked down and said, "For just coming out of boot camp, that was a pretty poor salute."

Private Ross, confused and in fear he had accidentally offended his new sergeant, snapped to a properly rigid posture and even though it forced him to squint into the bright sun, presented a textbook salute. He barked, "Sorry sir!"

Sarge had intended his comment to be more of a joke than a reprimand, so he was a bit surprised by the private's response. Trying to resettle Casey's nerves, the sergeant said, "Relax private. You're liable to pop a blood vessel standing that tight. Besides, I'm not really big on formality in this outfit. Just do what I tell you to do and we'll get along fine."

Assuming a more normal posture and breathing pattern, Private Ross scanned the cargo area and the strange faces peering back at him, like he were a lost puppy dog. Sarge motioned to a spot along the row of men and said, "Make some room for our new boy."

The men started shifting their gear, clearing the seat Sarge had indicated. Reaching over to grab the coat sleeve of one of the soldiers, Sarge said, "Ross. This guy here is Corporal Fletcher. We call him Doc. For the next couple of days, I want you to follow him around, at least until you can find your own way. Doc's been around for while and can show you the ropes."

Clumsily climbing over the tailgate, Casey stepped on more than one pair of feet before finding his seat on the bench. First nodding to Doc and shaking his hand, Casey returned his attention to Sarge, saying, "I'll do muh best to make you proud."

Sarge rolled his eyes and turned his attention out the back of the truck. He'd seen these greenies come and go. It seemed as if they were getting younger every time. They came here eager and stupid. In the front lines, most of them would go home cold and dead. In the back lines, such as they were, there weren't too many immediate dangers. Unlike many of the rookies he'd previously led into actual battle, this one would have time to learn how to survive.

The arrival of a new man to the unit was always an exciting time. Many of the men had been in the field for years, in for the duration as they said. Mail wasn't always quick in catching up with them, newspapers and magazines were often months old. New blood in the unit meant possible news from home, updates on what things were like in other battle theaters, and information not available from other sources. Sometimes, anything new was a welcome diversion.

In their eagerness, hands started reaching out from all directions, a half-dozen voices asking questions simultaneously. Combined with the noise of the truck and the road, it was nearly overwhelming and impossible to sort out. Corporal Fletcher stuck his arms between the welcomers like a boxing referee separating two fighters. "Reel those hooks back in boys. There will be plenty of time to ask all of your questions. While we're killing time here, why don't we get some introductions out of the way."

There was a collective agreement and the men settled back into their seats, adjusting their helmets and gear. Doc said, "So, let's start with the new guy. Tell us something about yourself."

"I don't know what to say."

The group jeered him a bit, feeling his answer to be pathetically weak. A few boos were uttered. Doc waved the group to silence and said, "Why don't you start with your name, where you're from, and what you were doing before the war?"

"Okay, I kin do that. Muh name is Casey Ross. I guess you'd say I'm from Sweetwater, Oklahoma. Actually, muh daddy owns a cattle ranch pretty much out in the middle of nowhere, but Sweetwater's the closest big town.

As far as what I was doing before I went in the Army, I was herding cattle for muh daddy."

Tinker piped up with, "We've got us a genuine cowboy here. I vote his official nickname be Cowboy. All in favor say 'Aye'."

The group unanimously yelled, "Aye!"

"The 'Ayes' have it. Congratulations Ross, your new nickname is Cowboy."

Casey thought about it for moment then asked, "Is it really necessary for me to have a nickname?"

Doc stepped in, saying, "I'm afraid it is Cowboy. I'm not sure where it started, but everyone in this unit has had a nickname. You either bring one with you and we adopt it, or like in your case, we stick you with one. Did you already have one you'd like us to consider?"

"No. Not really. I suppose Cowboy is fine. I kin get used to it. So, what's all your nicknames?"

Doc said, "Good idea. I'll start and then we'll see where this goes. My real name is Peter Fletcher. I'm from Alabama. They started calling me Doc because I'm a medic. Seemed a natural. Besides, I'd betcha almost every medic gets labeled as Doc. You already met Sergeant Cummings. Calling him Sarge seemed a natural too."

Cowboy asked, "What's his first name?"

Sarge's head snapped back around to give Doc a serious scowl. Doc saw the look and told Cowboy, "Well, I guess it really doesn't matter. We all call him Sarge and it's probably best you do too."

Relenting, Sarge said, "What the hell. You're going to find out anyway. My first name is Randolph." Then craning his neck so he could look over the group, he added, "Has anyone got a problem with that?"

Heads appropriately lowered or signaled 'no'. Doc split the silence by saying, "Why don't we start with Brownie over here?"

Casey about fainted when he heard the nickname and realized it was attached to the only Negro, a very large Negro, in the unit. He leaned over to Doc and whispered, "Did you all call him Brownie because he's colored?"

Brownie defended himself, knowing what the obvious question must have been. "Yeah. My nickname's Brownie, but it ain't entirely because I'm colored. You recognize this?"

Brownie held out a huge rifle. Aside from the sheer size of the gun, the bipod legs attached to either side of the barrel easily identified the weapon. "Yes I do. That's a Browning Automatic Rifle."

Brownie added, "You bet your sweet ass it is. When it gets tough out there and you need some heavy duty firepower, you'll be calling out for old Brownie to come save you."

"I wasn't meaning any disrespect or nothing. It's just I haven't been around too many colored folk, at least not out in Oklahoma."

"Well, okay then. Ain't your fault."

Cowboy was still uncomfortable with his error and tried to cover it with, "I'm really am sorry. Where are you from, anyway?"

"I'm from New York City, Harlem to be exact. My momma runs a diner there. She cooks some of the best fried chicken in the city. If you're ever in Harlem you'll have to stop in and try some." Brownie put down the big rifle and reached his hand out to shake Casey's, saying, "My name's Leroy Williams. Nice to knows you."

Casey hesitated a bit and then shook the large hand. When the two hands parted, another hand snaked its way to Casey. Shaking the hand vigorously, a voice said, "Nice to meet you Cowboy. My name's George Carter. They call me Moocher because I have this gift for finding things."

"Like what kind of things?"

"Oh, hey, all kind of things. I got contacts in other units. We trade things. You need something. You ask me. I can get it or I can find someone who can get it."

Another voice said, "You haven't been able to get me what I want."

Moocher snapped back, "Shut up, Tinker. We all know what you want."

Tinker crossed his arms and tried to ignore everyone. Casey asked Doc, "What's all that about? Who's Tinker?"

"I'm Tinker." He temporarily held his hand in the air, but quickly returned to his uncooperative posture.

Doc offered an explanation with, "His name is Bradley Lewis. We call him Tinker because it seems as if he can fix anything."

"That ain't the only reason to call him Tinker," added Moocher.

"What's he mean by that?" asked Casey.

Doc decided if Private Ross hadn't had much experience with Negroes in Oklahoma, he'd surely had no experience with homosexuals, so he tried to ignore it. Unfortunately Private Carletti butted in and provided a clue with, "It's short for Tinkerbell."

Lewis stood up, angrily saying, "You're always saying that, and I resent it. You're just jealous of me, that's all."

Standing up and grabbing his own crotch, Carletti said, "Yeah, well I got your jealousy right here."

"Cut the crap," snapped Sarge. "Your stories are breaking my heart. If you clowns can't keep it under control, I'm going to start breaking some heads. Got it?"

Carletti and Lewis returned to their seats, but still glared at each other. Casey leaned over and asked Doc, "What was that all about?"

"That was Anthony Carletti. He's the only one in the group who brought their own nickname and made it stick."

"What is it?"

"He wanted to be called Fingers. He claims his family is part of the Mafia back in New York."

"Are they?"

"Who knows, but when he told us his nickname and threatened to have each of us killed if he didn't get to keep it, we let him keep it. It was more important to him than it was to us."

Casey nodded acknowledgment, then continued, "Okay, but what's his beef with Tinker?"

Doc leaned over farther and whispered in his ear, "On your ranch, have you ever seen one bull trying to mate with another bull?"

When Casey nodded, Doc added, "When you see it going on, what do you call it?"

Casey's eyes got bigger and his voice got a little bit too loud when he said, "We don't call it anything. We just whip the shit out of the bull on top."

The group broke out laughing and Tinker, who probably figured out the subject matter gave them a dirty look. Doc asked Casey, "Okay, but what if one man tried to love another man?"

"You mean a faggot?"

"Yeah. Carletti thinks Tinker is queer."

"Is he?"

"Do you want to find out?"

"No, but he couldn't be here if he was. Could he?"

Tinker decided to defend himself. "You know what the Army does to queers? They throw them in prison. So even if I was, I wouldn't tell you. Fingers is just jealous because I have the body of a dancer while he's stuck with that hairy mass of gorilla flesh over there."

Before Fingers could stand up and fight back, Sarge barked, "Can we move on to someone else? I'm tired of this crap."

Doc thought for a moment, then pointed and said, "How about you, Red."

"My name is William Johnson and I'm from Boone, Iowa."

"Why do they call you Red?" asked Casey.

There were a few snickers from the group and more than one person who said, "Go on, Red. Show him why."

With a small, embarrassed smile and practiced grace, he removed his helmet to show off a fine, full head of bright orange hair. As the laughter died down, another of the men put out his hand to shake Casey's, saying, "I'm Corporal Bambridge. My first name is Walter. They call me Professor."

Casey looked into the corporal's face. There was a studious look about him and he wore glasses. "Are you a teacher or something?" he asked.

Returning to his seat and pulling out a pipe, he crossed his legs and placed the unlit briar in the corner of his mouth and mused, "No I'm not, but both of my parents are professors in Chicago. When I return home, I do plan to become a professor, hopefully a chemistry professor. I think I'd like to do research into some of these synthetic fibers we're starting to see."

Doc whispered to Casey, "Don't get him started. He'll never stop."

"Whose the last guy? The one sitting in the corner?"

Tinker chimed in, "Don't give him any mind. He's off in his own little world most of the time."

The figure in the corner rocked his head back, using the wall of the truck to lift the front of his helmet far enough to give Tinker a dirty look. Doc asked, "Jerome. What do you want Cowboy, here, to know about you?"

Without much emotion, he said, "You tell the story as well as I do, Doc. You can do it for me."

"Casey, this is Jerome Miller. His family is in the jewelry business back home in New York. He is a Jew, so we nicknamed him The Jew. If he doesn't seem too thrilled about things, it's because he's here in the back lines instead of up front killing Germans."

Cowboy asked, "Does he have something personal against the Germans?"

Now more animated, Jerome straightened up and stressed, "Nazis. I have nothing against the German people. It's the Nazis I hate."

"What's the difference?" asked Ross.

Many of the men knew what was coming. They only hoped this was the shortened version when Jerome started, "The Germans are nice, law-abiding people who build cuckoo clocks and brew beer. The Nazis are perverted creatures who use murder and torture to promulgate their own twisted version of the world."

Casey asked, "Isn't that why we're all here? Aren't we trying to stop the Germans, or the Nazis?"

"You may be here to stop the Germans. I joined up to kill as many Nazis as I can. The Nazis have been rounding up Jews, killing them, torturing them, and shipping them off to concentration camps. I couldn't just sit home and let them do that to my people, Jews who could be my relatives, my flesh and blood. I want to be up on the front killing Nazis, not back here in the rear, cleaning up after the real fighting is over."

Jerome finished his speech and sat back down into his seat. He was a bit more satisfied, and no one was going to encourage him to continue. Casey thought for a moment and then asked Doc, "Now that he mentioned it, what is it we do back here in the rear?"

Doc explained, “We provide a couple of very important functions. The first and most important function is to go through a newly liberated town or village and make sure all of the Germans have really left. We make sure there are no snipers lingering around. We make sure there are no booby-traps left behind. We also look for any abandoned munitions or unexploded bombs. We don't want any of our guys or the villagers to get hurt.”

“That seems safe enough...”

Sarge cut Ross off in mid-sentence with, “I knew it. Damn it, I knew it. They still don't teach you guys nothing in boot camp. This may seem simple enough, Cowboy, but I'll guarantee the first time you let your guard down, thinking this is some leisurely stroll, some Kraut's going to blow your brains out. You aren't here because we needed extra help. You're here because the last guy they sent, went home in a box. You better remember that.”

Sarge turned back to looking out the back of the transport, so Casey asked Doc, “Is it true, what he said?”

“Yeah it is. A couple of weeks ago, they sent us some greenhorn, like yourself.”

“Poor old, Porkie,” said Moocher, “didn't stand a chance.”

Casey asked, “What happened to him?”

Doc replied, “It was his second day with us. We were heading to the central square of the town we were clearing. He got ahead of us and before we could stop him, he walked right out into the square to wash his face in the fountain and fill his canteen. Next thing we knew, a shot rang out and he fell face first into the fountain. Later, when it was safe to get to him, we found he was shot through the head.”

Everyone lowered their head for a moment and then returned to business. Casey paused for a second and then asked, "You said there was a couple of good things we do here. What was the other?"

"That's the best one. We give the people their town back. For the most part, they love us. The Germans took over, kicked them out of their houses, and took whatever they wanted. When our troops come through and liberate these towns, they're often in more of a mess than when the Germans came in. Our helping to clean up their town shows goodwill and improves the morale of the people."

The truck lurched to a stop and Sarge released the chains on the tailgate, which slammed down. "Okay boys and girls, play time is over. Pick up your toys and let's get to work."

Chapter 3

The town of Mont du Lac was relatively untouched by the fighting necessary to wrestle it free of its German occupation. A few buildings suffered from artillery wounds and a few buildings showed the unmistakable signs of tank shells.

They'd seen so much of this. Archeologists find telltale clues in rocks and river banks the average person walks past obliviously. So it was with these men. They could tell the type of explosive by the tracks they left. Deep, almost circular craters were the footprints of aerial bombs. They dove deep into the earth before exploding.

Craters, more angular in shape, often with a spray pattern of destruction in front of them, were the signs of medium artillery lobbed in from the nearby hills. Tanks left unusual clues. Their rounds often poked a neat hole into one wall of a building, only to explode inside, destroying one or more floors, or blowing out the rear wall.

Apparently the Germans had left Mont du Lac with a minimum of resistance, sparing the town a lengthy fight. There was ample evidence of their occupation still hanging around. The hotel was decorated with banners and flags bearing the unmistakable Nazi swastika. Some of the villagers, who had remained, were beginning to remove the blood red adornments and feeding them to a bonfire in the center of the street.

Sergeant Cummings' men, with the assistance of some of the villagers, were rounding up abandoned weapons and piling them in front of a burned out bakery for later collection and disposal. The men were polite and friendly, but ever watchful. Occasionally, from other parts of the town being worked by similar teams, a few bursts of gunfire would remind them of the dangers still lurking about.

Midday brought one of the ancillary benefits of the work they were doing...food. Magically, it seemed, loaves of bread would appear along with bottles of wine. Women carrying baskets would bring lunch to the working townsfolk as well as treats for the soldiers. The GI's would share some of their rations of canned meat and beans, and an impromptu dinner party would begin.

"Drink up, Cowboy," urged Moocher.

"Is it like this every day?"

Wiping his lips with his sleeve, Private Carter replied, "Nah. Ain't like this every day, but there always seems to be something. Like we told you, these people love us."

"How about you, Professor?" asked Casey. "Are you going to chow down?"

Corporal Bambridge, standing with his carbine in a ready position, said, "Not right now, Cowboy. You go enjoy yourself. A couple of us need to stay on watch. Just promise to save me something."

Private Johnson came over with the plate of his mess kit piled high with canned beans and a half loaf of bread in one hand. His mess cup and utensils were in the other as he sat down next to Ross. "I have to say it's nice to see another face from the heartland. All these city boys can get to you after awhile."

"Yup. I know what you mean."

Swallowing a big spoonful of beans, Red said, "This Army chow's just about as good as home, yet all these city guys do is complain about it. Hell, half the time back home, we're so busy we forget all about lunch and don't get to eat until supper."

"Yup, I know what you mean."

Holding out his mess cup, Red asked, "Have you tried any of this wine?"

"Nope. I think I'll drink water. I ain't got much of a taste for wine."

Red chuckled a bit and then said, "I was that way too. Back home you got to be twenty-one before you can drink at a bar or buy liquor. Here, though, these Frenchies drink wine with everything. Hell, they even start the little kids out on it."

"They let kids drink the wine?"

"Yeah, they water it down, but they start the toddlers drinking wine."

Cowboy was a little surprised. He took a sip of water, then continued, "Back on muh daddy's ranch, they might let a twelve year old taste some beer just to watch him make a face, but we wasn't allowed to drink beer regular until we was eighteen. Things sure are different here."

Red asked, "You said your daddy had a cattle ranch, didn't you?"

"Yup. We got us twenty-five hundred acres of grazing land, plus some crop land."

"Twenty-five hundred acres? That's almost four square miles. I thought we had a big farm, but we ain't got half of what you have."

"You a farm boy, Red?"

"Hell yes. My family farms almost a thousand acres. We raise corn and wheat, and a few animals, mostly for our own use."

A shadow overcast the two, causing them to halt their conversation and look up to see who was standing in front of them. Fingers Carletti, holding a wine bottle in one hand, said, "What are you two rubes talking about?"

Red replied, "We're just talking about home and stuff. Nothing you'd be interested in."

"Damned straight I wouldn't be interested. You plowboys are just about the..."

Corporal Bambridge stiffened and trained his stare onto something in the distance. He cut off Carletti in mid-sentence by holding his palm up and speaking out an authoritative, "Shh!"

Slowly, everyone in the unit stopped their conversation and moved their attention to the Professor. Casey Ross, in a whisper, asked him, "What's got you spooked?"

The corporal lowered his hand and without moving his eyes from his target, he whispered back, "I'm not sure, but it's got me puzzling a bit."

Silently, Sarge slipped in behind Bambridge's shoulder and quietly asked, "What you looking at?"

"Well, Sarge, I wasn't sure at first, but the more I think this thing through, the fishier it seems."

"What are you talking about, Professor?"

"See those three guys over there pulling the cart?"

"Yeah, so they've got a load of debris and they're taking it out of town to dump it. What about it?"

By now, several of the men were also standing behind Sarge, trying to figure out what was so interesting. Bambridge was only slightly aware of them, keeping his attention focused on the trio of men. He said, "That was what I originally thought, but there were a few things which didn't fit."

"Like what?"

"For starters, look at the cart they're pushing. Most of the people around here have got two-wheel carts with big wooden wheels. These guys have got a steel cart with steel wheels and rubber tires. Looks a lot like a military cart, maybe an ammo cart."

Sarge thought for a moment, then said, "They could have found some leftover cart in the rubble."

"Yeah, I thought of that too, but then I looked inside the cart. That doesn't look like rubble to me. It doesn't even look haphazardly loaded. It looks a lot like someone moving their household goods."

Doc joined the conversation with, "Maybe their house got blown up and that stuff is what they could save and now they're moving it to a new home."

Bambridge said, "Yeah, I thought that too, but then I started looking at the three men. Almost everyone around here is elderly and the majority are women. What are the odds of three, healthy and strong, young men being left behind by the Krauts?"

Sarge said, "Could have happened. Not likely, but could've happened."

"I almost gave up there myself, but then I looked at the way they were dressed."

Sarge squinted his eyes as if he were trying to focus them better. He turned back to the Professor and said, "I don't see anything odd. They're wearing the same wear worn, wool coat and flannel pants as the other people.

They're also wearing the same stupid beret and scarf as half these other men, so what's the problem?"

"Look at their boots."

"What about their boots?"

"Most of the villagers wear those fabric shoes or brown leather boots which look as if they've been walking through manure. Take a good look at their boots."

The men were now too far away for Sarge to see clearly, so he pulled out a pair of binoculars. He focused them and noticed the men were wearing black leather boots and they were almost freshly shined. "Damn you've got good eyes, Professor. You think real good too."

Red asked, "What are we going to do, Sarge?"

Turning to the group, Sarge said, "Okay, let's allow them to get a little further out of the center of town. If something goes bad here, I don't want innocent bystanders getting in the way."

"What the hell are you talking about Sarge?" asked Fingers,

"There's three guys pulling a cart full of material out of town. It may be nothing, but Professor here thinks there's something fishy about them and I do too." Sarge knelt down and started to draw in the dirt as he continued, "Doc, you take Ross, Fingers, and Red. Cut over to the next street and run past those guys. Get up ahead of them and stand around like nothing's going on."

Doc said, "What are you boys going to do?"

"The rest of us are going to casually walk along behind these guys until we get closer to you, then we'll stop them. I'll start asking them questions and we'll see what they're up to. Doc, take your men and move out. The rest of you bums get your gear ready."

The men loitered for a few minutes to allow the others to reach their positions. Sarge started his men forward, saying, "In a few minutes, I want three of you to cross over to the other side of the street. I don't want to panic these guys. Stay sharp. Don't be too itchy on those triggers, and let me do the talking when we get there."

Trying to be casual in their approach, the groups gradually began to converge on the questionable trio laboring along, their cart of material in tow. Just outside of town, the trap closed, forcing the wagon pullers to stop. The men all stood staring at each other until Sarge asked, "Where are you fellows going with this?"

Shrugging their shoulders and appearing not to understand Sarge's question, the three kept looking around cautiously. The professor tried to be tricky, asking Sarge's question in German. "Wo gehen Sie?"

The trio reacted to the question initially, but quickly returned to their confused appearances. Sarge asked again, in his broken French, "Ou est-ce que marcher?"

The leader of the trio puzzled, then eventually figured out what Sarge was trying to say, smiled, and started rattling off an animated explanation in French, including extensive hand gestures. This apparent recognition and cooperation, momentarily eased the tension between the groups.

The two other wagon pullers started laughing, one brushing dirt from his jacket and the other adjusting the beret on his head. Brownie started to move forward, reaching for the canvas covering the contents of the wagon. The laughter strained and then stopped as Brownie's hand neared the cart.

A number of things happened within seconds of each other. The wagon puller who was dusting his jacket reached into his pocket, causing Cowboy to tighten the grip he had on his rifle. The trio's leader spun around and yelled "Nein", causing Sarge to realize all Hell was about to break loose.

The third member yelled, “Schwartze” and pushed Brownie away from the wagon. The man, whose hand had been in his pocket, pulled out a Luger handgun and leveled it toward Cowboy, who reflexively pulled the trigger on his rifle, instantly killing the threatening gunman.

The sound of the gunshot pumped adrenaline into the arteries of the other men. An instant later more shots rang out and the three strangers lay dead in the dust. The smoke of the gunfire slowly cleared and the report of the gunshots slowly echoed out of the men's ears. The men looked around. Nine were standing. Cowboy was slumped on the ground.

“Shit!” cried Sarge. “Some one check out Ross.”

Doc ran over and pulled Cowboy to a sitting position and quickly checked him over for wounds. Seeing none, he gently slapped Cowboy back to consciousness. Casey's eyes fluttered open, his face dripping sweat. Trying to collect his thoughts and steady his rapid breathing, he gasped, “Did I really shoot that guy?’

Doc looked into the still scared eyes and said, “Yes, Cowboy. You shot him. Are you all right?”

Cowboy was a confused mess of energy, emotion, and adrenaline. Part proud of himself, part ashamed, and part in shock, he struggled to his feet and said, “Yeah, I'm fine.” Then, looking down at the body of his victim, he fell back down to a sitting position, hanged his head, and said, “I take it back. I don't feel very good.”

Chapter 4

Townspeople, conditioned to the tragedies of war, heard the gunshots and momentarily paused from their work. They looked over the curious crowd of men on the side of the road. Satisfied the incident was finished and comfortable in the fact they were not involved, the townsfolk returned to their work.

Corporal Bambridge stood over one of the victims, taking note of the shiny black boots which proved to be the dead man's undoing. With the barrel of his gun, he pushed and prodded the body into a more dignified position. Rolled onto his back, the corpse's beret fell off, exposing a head of blond hair. The still open eyes were bright blue. "Hey Sarge. You should come and see this."

Satisfied Cowboy would survive his brush with death, Sarge spun around and walked over to Bambridge's side. "What you got, Professor?"

"What do you make of this?"

Sarge noticed the same peculiar items as Bambridge. He also noticed that in being rolled and pushed, one of the corpse's pant legs had worked its way up over the boot top. Another pair of black pants were underneath. "Damned strange," he said.

Looking further up the dead body, on the man's lapel, the Professor noticed the shiny, back clasp of a pin. Using the barrel of his rifle to pull the lapel backward, he found another clue to the puzzle. Sarge looked at the pin, patted the Professor on the back and said, "You sure pegged these guys. Nice job, corporal."

By now, a couple of the other men had gathered with them. A few recognized the pin, but it fell to Fingers to ask, "Nice jewelry. What is it?"

Doc answered, "Totenkopf."

"What in the hell is that?" demanded Carletti.

"Death's Head," said the Jew. Jerome's answer startled everyone for a second. He hardly ever volunteered. Even more chilling, was he said it matter of factly, coldly, similar to a tour guide's presentation of some museum piece.

Ross had managed to get back up on his feet and work his way over to the group. He asked, “What's this Death's Head?”

The Jew answered, “It's the symbol of the Schutzstaffel.”

Cowboy said, “I've never heard of this shoots table or whatever you said.”

“You may know them as the SS. Heinrich Himmler's elite troops, the Stormtroopers. These guys are the truly hard core Nazis.”

Sarge thought out loud, “I wonder what a group of SS thugs were doing, pushing a cartload of rubbish.”

Doc decided some action was necessary to begin cleaning up the spectacle. He motioned toward some nearby trees and said, “Lewis, Williams, and Carletti. Each of you grab one of these bodies and drag it over to those trees. Sarge, I'll go with them and search the bodies.”

Nodding agreement, Sarge said, “That sounds like a good idea. Let me know if you find anything of interest.”

Walking over to the cart, Sarge pulled back one part of the canvas cover, motioned for the Professor to pull back another part of it, and said, “Let's take a look see and find out what was so important.”

A number of the men came to their assistance and started to rummage through the material carefully piled in the cart. Exposed, the contents indeed appeared to be someone moving their household. Everything was neatly packed and arranged. The cart was filled with trunks, suitcases, and wooden crates. Slowly, the men pulled out containers and examined their contents.

“All I got in this trunk is uniforms, clothes, and stuff,” said a disappointed Moocher as he rummaged through a large travel case.

Red and Casey opened a wooden crate and found a dozen rifles, some ammunition, and handguns. Jerome and Bambridge opened a large crate and found a portable desk, some books, files, and other paraphernalia consistent with a field office.

Doc returned with his three pall bearers, his hands filled with wallets and papers. "What did you find out?" asked Sarge.

Doc handed the material to Sarge and then explained, "Seems they were SS all right."

"What were they doing pushing this cart?"

"Well, near as I can tell, the guy you were talking to was a colonel. At least that's what his papers say, and that's assuming my weak German is accurate."

"Who were the other two?"

"They must have been his aides or maybe lieutenants."

Sarge shuffled through the papers, seeming to be satisfied with the information Doc had gleaned from them. "Okay, so we know who they are, but we still don't know why they were still here and what they were doing with this cart. Why did an SS colonel stay behind?"

"He'd set himself up as the Mayor," interrupted Corporal Bambridge.

Sarge turned around to see the Professor holding a book in his hand. Bambridge had the book open and apparently was reading out of it. "Where did you come up with that?" Sarge asked Walter.

Gently waving the book in the air, he said, "I found his journal."

Looking at the handwriting in it, Sarge asked, "Can you make sense out of this German chicken-scratch?"

Peering over the rims of his glasses with a look of disdain, the corporal stared at Sarge, until Sarge realized the insinuation. “My German is just fine,” added the Professor. “Now, do you want to know what's in here?”

Sarge wasn't going to be bullied, so he said, “Don't get a big head, Mr. Know-it-all. You don't know what I meant. Just fill in the holes for us.”

“Seems this Colonel Hamill was put in charge of the occupation in this area. He decided to take it one step further and set himself up as Mayor or more like a Prince. There are notes in here, documenting the bribes and taxes he demanded and collected.”

The men who heard this story, assumed the money was still in the cart and quickened their search through it. The redoubling of efforts was easily noticed, but Sarge had no interest in slowing them down.

Corporal Bambridge dampened their enthusiasm when he said, “Before you guys get too excited, these records also show he used couriers to deliver the money to some banks in Switzerland, so I don't expect you'll find much in the wagon.”

Work slowed and a collective groan of disappointment was heard. As the stack of material grew smaller, it became necessary for one of them to climb into the cart and pull items out for distribution. Moocher volunteered for the job. Box after box left the wagon until the last layer was exposed. Reaching into the corner of the cart, Private Carter called out, “Hey everyone. Get a load of this.”

He stood up and jumped out of the cart, a wooden box in his arms. The men left their tasks and crowded around Moocher to see what he had found. He was holding a small, wooden chest. It appeared to be very old, the wood darkened by age and handling.

The chest was made of oak, about fifteen inches long and about ten inches square on the other sides. The lid was attached with heavy wrought iron hinges. Other wrought iron bands reinforced the box's walls, being held in place with large iron rivets and nails. A hasp, held the lid in place with a large, very old padlock.

Sarge and Bambridge fought their way into the front of the crowd. "Looks like you found the money pot," said Sarge.

Everyone stood staring at the box for a few minutes, turning it over and around, admiring the craftsmanship and age of the piece. Tinker asked, "Hey, what's the stuff on the lid?"

Moocher looked at it closely and said, "Looks like one of those coat of arm things. You know like the knights of old, when men were bold." Everyone chuckled at the joke.

Sarge suggested, "I think we've seen enough of the outside. Let's get a look at what's inside." Sarge took the chest from Carter's hands, looked at the lock and joked, "Has anyone got the key?"

Private Carletti offered his bayonet and said, "I got your key."

Sarge took the knife and tried prying the lock open, levering the shackle with the blade. Seeing him have no luck in opening the lock, someone suggested, "Why don't you just shoot it open?"

Doc pushed his way forward saying, "Maybe one of these will work?" He held out a large key ring with at least twenty oddly shaped and sized keys hanging from it.

"Where did you get these?" asked Sarge.

"I took them off of the colonel when I searched him."

Sarge first examined the ring of keys, trying to see if any of them obviously looked like it fit the lock. Seeing none, he started trying one after the other. More than one of the bystanders added their suggestions as to which key to try next. Finally, one of them worked. Turning around in the hole, the shackle popped open with a loud clacking sound. With a collective cheer from the crowd, Sarge said, "We have a winner!"

The cheering quickly died down as they waited for the sergeant to open the box. He pulled the lock out of the hasp and had to apply considerable effort to get the rusted hasp to lift out of the way. When he opened the box, it at first appeared to be empty. Eventually he realized he was looking at a black velvet bag.

Sarge pulled out the bag and handed the box to one of the men. Slowly he looked for the opening. He slowly pulled back the cloth. The group gasped in amazement as the sunshine exploded off the golden item within, and Sarge's eyes widened when he slowly whispered, "Holy shit."

The sergeant shook his head to regain his senses and quickly recovered the object, held it close to his chest and looked around to see if anyone else saw the item. Sarge tucked the bag under one arm and started off toward the trees. He said, "Some of you guys start loading up the cart so it looks just like we found it. Drag the cart over to the trees where we put the Krauts. After that, meet me over by the other clump of trees. The rest of you guys come with me. I don't think we should be showing this thing around."

The men filled the wagon and threw the canvas back over it, but they didn't do the neat and tidy job the sergeant had ordered. It now looked like the pile of rubble they had first suspected. They quickly rolled it near its previous owners and then ran over to where Sarge was sitting under one of the trees.

Sarge waited until all ten men were assembled and then looked around for other prying eyes. Seeing no one else, he carefully removed the black bag, exposing the golden chalice it contained. "Will you look at this," he said.

Many of the men whistled at the sight of the heavy, gold drinking cup. Sarge dropped the black bag and hefted the cup, taking note of the weight. “It must be made of solid gold,” he said in awe.

“Take a look at all those jewels,” sighed the Moocher.

Sarge looked around the group, found the Jew, and said, “Jerome. Take a look at this. Are these things real?”

Miller carefully took the chalice in his hands and peered deeply into the colored stones. He held them so he could see light through them. He tapped the metal of the cup, making a heavy and dull ringing sound. He handed the cup back to Sarge and said, “I can't tell for sure, at least not without a magnifying glass and some other tools, but they seem real to me.”

Fingers offered, “It must be worth a fortune.”

“Sarge? ” asked Cowboy. “I know I'm the new guy and such, but what do we do when we find things like this?”

No one had thought of that question. The men started looking at each other. They knew they were supposed to turn in valuable items to the civil authorities or to the battalion commander, but this was different. After thinking about it for a few seconds, everyone suddenly started offering their opinions.

“Let's sell it.”

“Tear the jewels off of it and divide them between us all.”

“Melt it down.”

Sarge cut off the discussion with, “Knock it off! I'll tell you what we're going to do.” Everyone listened and watched as Sarge re-wrapped the chalice in its velvet bag, placed it back in the chest, closed the lid and said, “First off, all of you dog faces are sworn to secrecy. I will personally rip out the tongue of the first one of you who opens his mouth. You guys understand?"

Everyone nodded agreement and listened to Sarge say, "Bambridge, you call Battalion and tell them we caught three Krauts trying to steal a bunch of stuff. Tell them they put up a fight and we had to kill them. Tell them where to find the cart and the bodies. Got it?"

Professor nodded and said, "Tell them to pick up the trash. Got it."

The sergeant looked around for something. Not finding what he needed he said, "Red. Run and get your field pack. Bring it back here."

Private Johnson dropped his rifle and equipment belt, and ran like the wind to retrieve his pack. Casey still wanted his question answered when he asked, "I thought we were supposed to turn this stuff in. Isn't that what we're going to do, Sarge?"

Fingers spun around and hissed, "Shut up, plow boy."

Sarge had a similarly greedy but more logical response. "We can always turn this thing in when the time comes, Cowboy. On the other hand, we have no idea who this belonged to or where it came from. Wouldn't it make more sense to get it back to the rightful owner?"

"That makes sense, Sarge, but how are we going to find out?"

About this time, Red came running up with his pack. "Empty out the damned thing, and then hand it to me," Sarge said.

Red dumped out the contents, some of which the sergeant scooped up. Wrapping the chest in some clothes and a blanket, Sarge stuffed the material into the pack and closed it. He stood up and slung the pack over one shoulder. He told the waiting group, "Let's go back into town, get our gear, and call it a day. We've had enough excitement for one day."

The crowd began to spread out and walk into the village. Doc worked his way up to the sergeant's shoulder, and as they walked along, he casually asked, "Have you got a game plan here or are you making this up as you go?"

"We've got four days of stand down time to figure out what to do. I don't want someone else, either these Frenchies or the Army, getting their paws on this thing until we've had time to sort it out ourselves."

"You know we're breaking some heavy-duty Army regulations here. We could all go to prison."

"I know that. You know that. But, do you want to tell it to these guys right now?"

"No. I suppose not."

"That's my point. Let's sneak this thing out of town and back to our camp. We've got four days to decide. If we decide to turn it in, it won't matter if it's today, tomorrow, or the day after tomorrow."

Chapter 5

The glow from the fire, brightly lit the faces of ten young men, soldiers who formed a solemn circle around the glowing embers. Each searched their own conscience for an answer of what to do with the treasure fate placed in their custody. Each had their own idea, but was reluctant to share it with the group.

"How in the hell do we know the thing is even real?" asked one of the young men.

Moocher said sarcastically, "Why don't you take it to a jeweler and ask for an appraisal?"

"Oh, I think it's real," opined Sarge. "Why else would an SS Colonel take such risks? Nothing else in the wagon was worth killing for."

Casey Ross was still doing the honest thing when he said, "I know you don't want to hear this, but I say we turn it in to Battalion."

"This ain't a few hundred dollars we're talking about," said Moocher. "This is a king's fortune. That cup is worth ten thousand bucks if it's worth a dime."

The Jew spoke with experienced confidence when he said, "It's at least tens of thousands of dollars. It could even be worth a hundred thousand bucks."

The size of the fortune sunk into the minds of the men and caused a pause of silence. Several of the men muttered and whistled, "A hundred thousand bucks. Imagine that."

"All the more reason to turn it into the Army," re-asserted Cowboy.

"Shows what you know plowboy," offered Carletti.

"What do you mean?"

Fingers tried to explain his position with, "Who're you going to turn it over to? If you were some poor sap working the front desk at Battalion and this dropped in your lap, wouldn't you be tempted to keep it yourself?"

Cowboy saw the logic, but said, "So you ask to see an officer and turn it in to them."

Sarge said sarcastically, "What makes you think an officer is any more honest than a clerk?"

"Yeah, this German was a colonel and he was certainly padding his nest with money and stuff. What makes you think our officers are any more honest than theirs?" noted Doc.

Cowboy, still trying to do the right thing, said, "So take it to the General if you have to."

"The point is, no matter who we give it to, someone will eventually keep it. Why shouldn't it be us?" asked the Moocher. There was considerable agreement by the group to the comment.

The Professor tried to bring some logic to the discussion by saying, "Let's put aside the decision as to whether or not we turn the chalice in. For the sake of argument, let's say we're going to keep it. What do we do with it?"

Everyone started looking at the others with puzzled looks. They'd been so intent on possessing it, they failed to consider how they might have to share it, or if they could share it.

Brownie suggested the first solution with, "I say we pry off all of those jewels and divide them up between all of us."

Tinker asked, "How do we do it fairly?"

Sarge offered comically, "I say we go by rank." The joke was not received well by the group. No one laughed.

Jerome suggested, "I don't think there is a fair way of dividing the individual stones. Besides that, I personally think the cup would be significantly more valuable in one piece. Jewels are jewels, and gold is gold, but an object of art is unique. There may also be some historical value to it we don't even know about."

Carletti groused, "You're thinking like the Jew you are. Greedy to the bitter end."

"What in the Hell is your problem, Carletti?" chastised Moocher. "He's got a point, a damned good point as far as I'm concerned. What's wrong with him telling us how to get more money for this thing?"

"It's a stupid point," said Fingers holding his open palm in the air and waving it toward Moocher in a go away gesture.

"What's stupid about it?" asked Red.

"Hey, I ain't denying the fact this thing may be worth more in one piece. That part makes sense. The problem is, how are you going to unload it in one piece?"

"I still don't get what you're saying," said Red.

"The Jew said objects of art are unique. Don't you think anyone we try to sell this thing to will recognize it?"

Once again, an obvious problem the group had failed to consider, made itself known. Another round of thinking began. Another round of ideas were hatched. Brownie returned to his original idea, saying, "I still sez you pry the jewels off it and melt down the gold. I'm willing to take my share of say twenty thousand dollars and getting away with it, instead of a hundred thousand and getting caught."

"I'm beginning to like his idea," said Tinker, "but how are we going to divide the stuff?"

Moocher spoke up with, "I don't want to be a party pooper or nothing, but I do think I should remind you all that I found the chest, so I think I deserve the most."

"Where in the Hell did that come from? Who do you think you are?" questioned Tinker.

"Hey. I was the one who found it. I didn't have to tell any of you guys. I could have kept it for myself."

"Bullshit, Moocher," spewed Fingers. "With your logic, we should give Doc most of it because he found the key to open it."

The Professor added, "For that matter, I deserve it most because I spotted the Germans in the first place."

"Shut up, you clowns," barked Sarge. "I am not going to stand for this kind of crap. There's got to be some way to do this, so stop fighting over who gets what, and figure out some way to fix this."

Private Miller suggested, "If we could find some way to ship it home to my family, they could piece it out, sell the components, and then we could share the money."

"Not a bad idea," replied Tinker, "but no offense intended, how can we trust you and your family?"

Fingers said angrily, "I don't know about you guys, but I ain't trusting a bunch of Jews with this much money. I guarantee you they'd find some way to screw us."

"Fuck you," was Jerome's answer to Carletti's insults.

Fingers wasn't about to apologize, but he tried to soften it with, "It ain't nothing personal, but you all know how Jews are with money. They ain't going to want to let go of a dime they don't have to. By the time they got done playing with the records and such, how would any of us know we hadn't been cheated?"

"Fuck you again."

Sarge butted in again saying, "I told you guys to keep this shit under control. Unless one of you guys comes up with a better idea, I say we hang onto it, in one piece, until we figure out what to do."

The Professor, who was quietly watching the exchange of viewpoints, entered the discussion with, "I may have an interesting solution to our dilemma."

"What's on your mind?" asked Sarge.

"Well it seems to me there are three things we need to figure out. The first is what this thing is and whether or not there is any art value to it."

"I follow your logic," concurred Tinker, "but what's the other two?"

"The second problem is regardless of the cup's value and how we plan to dispose of it, we need someone to sell it to here, or at least figure out some way to smuggle it home. You know darn well the Army will search us when we go home. As it is, they search our mail and packages now."

Once again, an unforeseen obstacle was placed in the path of the men and their pot of gold. Tinker eventually said, "I'm sure the Professor here has figured out a solution and I'll bet it brings us to the third problem."

"Absolutely. If we keep this chalice, in one piece or many, sell it here or send it home, we need someone locally we can trust. We need someone whose opinion and advice we can rely on."

Tinker could wait no longer and asked, "Who do you have in mind?"

"Marie."

Sarge realized the corporal had found the right answer. He said, "You're absolutely right, Bambridge. We can trust Marie and we've still got the four days off. We've got plenty of time to get her opinion. Moocher, can you get us a truck?"

Insulted slightly, Moocher said, "Do you really have to ask? Of course I can get us a truck."

Sarge stood up and grabbed the chest containing the golden cup. "Okay everyone, get some shut eye. I want to be on the road by zero seven hundred."

"Who's this Marie person?" Casey asked Red.

"It'd take too long to explain right now, but trust me, you'll see."

Chapter 6

Seven o'clock arrived at the same time as any other morning, but never had these men been so eager to greet its arrival. Most hardly slept at all that night. Of the others who could sleep, most spent a restless night of tossing and turning. One of the men, Tinker, had no trouble sleeping. In fact he spent his evening dreaming of what he would do with his share of the treasure. On the long truck ride to Marie's chateau, he decided to regale his captive audience with his account.

"I have always wanted to own my own theater," he told the others. "I'd constantly have different things playing there. I'd have ballet and concerts for the highbrows. I'd have plays and big bands for the average man. On Saturday mornings, I'd put on shows for the children."

"So what was this dream you had last night?" asked Red.

"It was wonderful," squealed Tinker wrapping his arms around himself in an embrace. "My theater was doing a stage version of that recent movie, The Wizard of Oz."

"And I suppose you was playing Dorothy," taunted Fingers.

"As a matter of fact, I wasn't," was Tinker's reply, accented with a nasty look. "I was playing the Cowardly Lion."

"Yeah. Right. Like that's tough for you," huffed Carletti.

Tinker gave up on describing his dream and said to Fingers, "At least I have dreams, things I want to accomplish. Have you made plans for your share? That is, if we figure out how to get shares."

"As a matter of fact, I have been thinking what I'd do. I'd go back to New York and start a small construction business, you know, building them tract homes. There's going to be a lot of houses being built after the war's over and I want to get in on the action."

Tinker couldn't resist a dig and said, "That's about as imaginative as I'd expect some Dago to be."

Moocher, who was driving the truck, almost forgot a turn on the tricky route to Marie's home. It had been a couple of long months since he'd driven it, and in order to make the turn he hit the brakes rather hard. In the middle of the turn, the truck came precariously close to rolling over. Men were tossed around the cargo area, effectively ending the dispute of the two quarreling men.

"Sorry about that!" shouted Moocher through the open rear window, to the men in back.

"Watch where you're going, you moron," yelled back Doc. "Are you trying to get the cup for yourself by killing all of us?"

"Hey, what about you, Doc?" asked Red. "Have you thought about what you'd do with the money?"

"It would certainly pay for my medical schooling and maybe even have enough left over to help me open my own office. What about you, Red?"

"Hell, I can't even imagine how much money it would be. That's more money than I dreamed I'd ever see in my lifetime. I don't know what I'd do."

"He'd probably go out and buy himself some pigs," teased Brownie, adding some oinks and gestures to make sure everyone knew he was joking around.

Red laughed along with everyone else, being used to their kidding about his country upbringing. After a second thought, he reminded the group, "You guys ain't got just me to joke around with anymore. Remember we got Cowboy here."

"Yeah. That's right," mused Brownie. "What things have you been thinking about doing with your part of the money, Cowboy?"

Cowboy tilted his helmet back on his head and said, "I know you guys are tired of hearing me say this..."

In unison, the group finished his sentence, "I think we should turn the cup in to the authorities."

Embarrassed by the laughter which was added, he sulked and said, "Well, I do think that."

The Professor came to Cowboy's assistance for the first time, saying, "Cowboy, I actually agree with you. I wish we could turn it in, but I also see how foolish it would be."

"Yeah, man," added Brownie. "If we don't keep it, the next guy along the chain will, or the one after him. Eventually, someone's going to get rich, so why shouldn't it be us?"

This was the tenth time the men had been through this and the logic, although twisted to a certain extent, was accurate. Spoils of war, after all, are spoils of war. Somebody wins and somebody loses.

Brownie continued by saying, "For me, I'd go back to Harlem and pay off my momma's debts and hire her some help so she could slow down some. She's been getting up at the crack of dawn, working her fingers to the bone until all hours of the night, to provide for us children. I think I'd buy her some rest."

Jerome said, "I know who I'd buy some rest for."

Surprised at his participation in the conversation, Brownie asked, "Who'd you help?"

The Jew said, "I'd take my money and invest it."

"Said like a true Jew," poked Carletti.

"Sit on it Carletti. I'd invest the money and use the interest to run an agency to reunite families separated by the war. We'd help do research to find out what happened to their families and help provide money to bring them to America."

Everyone was surprised by this generous side to Miller. There was a moment of silence and then Carletti said, "I apologize, Jerome. That sounds like a truly noble cause. What else would your agency do?"

"We'd also provide the manpower and money to hunt down every Nazi pig, slit their throats, and watch them bleed like a Kosher animal."

"That's the Jew we all know and love," applauded Sarge. "We're going to be there in about half an hour.

Now I don't want anyone talking to Marie about the cup except me. You got it?" Everyone nodded.

Doc asked, "What should we tell her when she asks why we just dropped in on her like this?"

"You can tell her the truth. We got an extra couple of days off, so we thought we'd come visit our old friend, Marie."

"So what's the big worry, Sarge. We can trust Marie. Why don't you just ask her?" quizzed Red.

"I know we can trust her, but something this big needs to be handled differently. Let me feel her out a bit. With any luck, she may come up with a solution without us even having to tell her what the item is."

"How are you going to do that?"

"You know, maybe I'll tell her it's some valuable painting or something. I won't give her any of the details as to how we got it. I'll just ask her how we'd go about selling it."

"That isn't going to work," said the Professor.

"And why not?"

"Because she is going to have to see it. A famous painting can not be pieced out or melted down. This thing can. A famous painting would only be of interest to collectors at an auction or a private sale, both of which would cause people to ask how we got a hold of it."

"The Professor's got a good point there," chimed in Tinker.

Sarge thought for a moment, realizing they were getting close to the road to Marie's home. "Okay, so we tell her and show her, but only after I say so. We leave the chest in the back pack. I'll get her alone and talk to her about it, as if we'd seen someone else with it. Then I'll decide whether or not to show it to her, and to ask for her advice."

Those issues settled for the time being, the men quietly waited out the remaining few minutes of travel. They heard and felt Moocher apply the brakes, slowing the truck sufficiently to make the right hand turn through the stonewall arch which marked the steep road leading up the hill to Marie's home. As Moocher shifted the truck into low gear, desperately double clutching the grinding gears, Sarge called out, “Okay boys, next stop, Chateau Remarque.”

Chapter 7

Private Ross was fortunate enough to have gotten one of the two seats at the tailgate of the truck. He admired the scenery as the truck labored up the hill. Casey noticed what once must have been extensive gardens with manicured lawns. The obvious signs of neglect were present, but at one time, the grounds must have been magnificent.

He could not see the house they were approaching, but based upon some of the statuary, walkways, and landscaping they passed, he had developed an image in his mind. The truck pulled into the circular drive in front of the house and came to a stop with the rear of the transport facing the entrance of the home. What Cowboy saw, did not disappoint him at all.

The building was huge. There was some minor battle damage, but the overall beauty of the estate was still evident. The main entrance was covered by a large portico, and steps led to the doors. Cowboy whistled and said, “Holy cow.”

“Something else isn't it?” commented Doc.

After stepping down from the transport, Cowboy asked Doc, “One person lives in this whole thing?”

"No. It used to be a country hotel, what the French call a l'auberge."

Casey looked around and asked, "Where are we anyway?"

Doc laughed a little and said, "Basically we're out in the middle of nowhere. That's the point. We're a good two hours from Paris, so when the well-to-do wanted to get away from the city, they'd come to a place like this."

"So who is this Marie person?"

The rest of the men were almost completely out of the truck now. Sarge was one of the last, making sure the chest inside of the backpack was secure, and then making sure the closure on the pack was secure.

Doc saw this and said to Cowboy, "I'll explain more to you later, but for now you just need to know her father used to own and run this place before the war. Now she's virtually by herself."

Sarge threw the pack over his shoulder and said, "Moocher. You got the other bag?"

Holding out the heavy duffel bag, using both hands, he replied, "Got it right here Sarge. Enough stuff for a really great party."

Sarge waved the men forward and started walking to the front door. Cowboy looked at the house and saw a lone figure peering through one of the windows on the second floor. The curtains fell back to their hanging position and a few moments later, the female figure appeared in the open doorway of the house.

The men reached the bottom of the steps and the woman held out her open arms and said, "What a surprise this is. My favorite American soldiers have dropped by to pay me a surprise visit."

The men, in near unison, cheered, "Marie."

When he got to the top of the stairs, Sarge and Marie hugged and she kissed each of his cheeks in the traditional French greeting. “It's been a long time, Marie.”

“Far too long,” cooed Marie. Taking one of Sarge's arms in hers to act as a guide into the home, she motioned for the others to follow and then said over her shoulder, “You men should know better than to leave a woman all alone for so long.”

The men filed into the foyer of the hotel and started to make themselves at home, placing their weapons and possessions around the entryway and then seeking out a convenient chair or sofa to sit. That is, everyone but Cowboy, who stood in the door like a lost child.

Marie released her hold on Sarge and strolled toward Casey. She bowed slightly, waving her arm in welcome, saying, “Pardon moi. These men I know, but your face is new. I am Marie Renee Remarque and I welcome you to my home.”

Still very confused, Cowboy realized he was still wearing his helmet. He quickly pulled his helmet off, put it under one arm, and mumbled out, “Howdy Ma'am. I'm Private Casey Ross.”

Turning back to Sarge, she asked, “He is new? No?”

“He's been with us only a couple of days now.”

She slowly walked around Private Ross making him quite nervous. She asked him, “And where are you from?”

Swallowing, he said, “I'm from Oklahoma, Ma'am.”

Sarge tried to help out by offering, “We've nicknamed him Cowboy because his family owns a cattle ranch.”

Marie giggled a little and moved closer to Ross, she stroked his chin and cheeks with her hand and said, “I thought cowboys were rough and tough, but this boy's face is not rough. How old are you?”

Cowboys face was about as red as a tomato. He was not comfortable with Marie's flirtatious manner and he stuttered out, "I'm n-n-nineteen, M-m-ma'am."

Realizing she had embarrassed him, she backed off and resumed her humble posture. She offered, "Later, I will make it a point of giving you the grand tour, but for now, come on in and make yourself at home."

Returning to the center of the foyer's circle, she held out her hands and spun slightly while saying, "As always, to all of you, you are welcome to stay as long as you can. My home is your home. Welcome to you all."

Sarge took the bag from Moocher and dragged it over to Marie. He started to open it and said, "I know you say we don't need to bring you anything when we visit, but we thought you might be able to use a few things."

Looking into the bag briefly, she patted Sarge on the cheek and said, "That was very sweet of you. How long can you stay?"

"We can stay a couple or three days, then we need to get back."

Excited by the prospects of the longer than normal visit, she recomposed herself and then said, "You must all be hungry from your trip. Would a couple of you help me take this to the kitchen? I'll be back shortly with some refreshments."

Sarge, Moocher, and Tinker headed off to the kitchen with Marie, leaving the others to lounge around the main hall of the hotel. Doc sought out Cowboy and said, "She's quite a woman isn't she?"

"No doubt, but what's going on here?"

Looking around, Doc suggested, "Drop your gear anywhere, and let's go into the library. These guys know the story, so there isn't any reason to bore them with a repeat. Besides, I think they're all going to catch some shut-eye."

Cowboy placed his gear near one of the tables and followed Doc down the hallway, past a ballroom, through the dining room, and into the southern end of the building. He opened the large double doors of the library and walked inside. The room was tall, maybe as much as twelve feet, but the actual size of the floor wasn't very large. Three of the walls were covered with shelves filled with books, a pair of portable ladders allowed access to some of the higher shelves. The fourth wall was consumed by several large windows which allowed a large amount of light to enter and illuminate the reading areas.

"I just love this room," said Doc. "Don't you?"

Cowboy was staring skyward, slowing turning around to survey the room and its contents. Eventually he replied, "I don't think the whole public library in Sweetwater has got this many books in it."

Doc motioned to a seating area near the windows, which allowed a good view of the pond behind the building. Doc lounged back into a large leather chair and Cowboy settled on a small divan. "So, who is this Marie woman? Is she a prostitute?"

"No. No. It isn't anything like that. I told you this used to be hotel."

"Yeah, you're right. I forgot about it."

Doc relaxed and laughed, "That's okay, boy, you wouldn't be the first to forget something after meeting Marie."

Cowboy smiled an embarrassed grin, fondly felt his cheek where Marie had caressed it, and then said, "So tell me the story of how you all got to know her."

"Well it all came about many months ago, maybe nearly a year. Sarge was part of the front line forces then. He was part of the force which liberated this part of France, actually routing the Germans out of the area. I sometimes think Sarge misses those times."

"Why isn't he still up on the front?"

Doc repositioned himself in the chair and then said, "Actually, these two stories are tied together."

"How's that?"

"Marie's family ran this hotel before the war. After the German's came through, the Krauts decided to occupy this area and use the hotel as sort of a resort for their officers."

"Is that why there isn't a lot of damage to the place?"

"I'm sure it is. The German officers like to live the high life, especially at the expense of their conquered populace, so they weren't going to let too much happen to this place. Anyway, as Marie tells it, her parents didn't mind it so much. I'm sure she hated the Germans, but they treated her family fairly well, and serving the elite of French society isn't much different than serving the elite of the Third Reich."

"So, they just went along with things?" asked Ross.

"Wouldn't you?"

"I don't know." Ross thought for a second or two and then asked, "So what changed things?"

"When the Allies invaded and the German's started to retreat, some of them were looking for people to blame. Marie's brother was executed by the Gestapo after being accused as a spy."

"Was he a spy?"

"It doesn't matter. If the Gestapo thinks you are, that's enough. A few days later, as the Allies were getting close to this area, the German soldiers turned on their hosts."

"What did they do?"

Pointing to one of the small sheds on the property, Doc said, "Marie's father was accused of collaborating with the French Underground and shot in the back of the head, near one of those sheds over there. Marie's mother was accused of poisoning some soldiers and killed."

Cowboy asked, "How is it Marie is still alive?"

"That's where Sarge comes into the picture. To make a long story short, his unit was assigned to clearing this property. The last of the Germans were doing their dirty work when the Americans arrived."

"Were you with Sarge then, Doc?"

"No, in fact no one else in the unit was with Sarge then. Anyway, Sarge heard some screams from one of the rooms and burst in on a couple of German lieutenants beating and raping some girl."

"Was the girl Marie?"

"Sure was. The Krauts had her tied down to a bed and were having their way with her when he broke in. For some reason, which came back to haunt him, Sarge didn't kill them right then and there."

Cowboy puzzled, "How did that come back to haunt him?"

"A couple of Sarge's men held the Krauts at gun point, while he untied the woman, I mean Marie. She held on to him tightly and when he untied the gag in her mouth, she sobbingly told him about what happened to her family and the terrible things she had endured."

"What did Sarge do to them?"

Doc shook his head in disgust and then said, "That's how his trouble with the Army started. After Marie told him what had happened, you can imagine how angry he must have been. Marie pleaded for him to kill the Germans."

"Seems like a reasonable request to me."

"Sarge walked over to the Krauts, who you can imagine by now, are pleading for their lives. While his men held the Germans at bay, Sarge beat the living daylights out of them, then he pulled his pistol out and killed them both."

Casey was confused and asked, "So how did Sarge get in trouble for that?"

"Well, after he put his pistol away, he turned around and found his lieutenant standing in the doorway. Apparently he'd seen most of the beating and felt Sarge had gone too far, particularly when he shot the Krauts."

"Did the lieutenant try to court martial him?"

Doc nodded and said, "Yeah he did. The lieutenant was new and trying to make a name for himself, so he was pushing the rules pretty hard. Fortunately, headquarters was pretty sympathetic to Sarge's decision and they worked out a compromise."

"What happened?"

"In exchange for not pressing the charges, Sarge was reassigned to this clean-up duty in the rear areas."

Casey shook his head and said, "Kind of a strange deal."

"All kinds of strange things go on in wartime. If Sarge would have busted into the room and blasted the Krauts right away, they would have pinned a medal on his chest. As it turned out, Sarge had to cool his heels for a while and he was able to spend a lot of time out here with Marie, helping her put her life back together again."

"Did Marie inherit the hotel then?"

"Yeah she got the place, but it was a long time before she was really ready to handle running the place."

"So how did the rest of you get to know her?"

Doc explained, "When Sarge got his new unit, the Army thought it would be great public relations for him to help Marie get her place back in shape."

"Were any of you guys with Sarge then?"

"Myself, Professor, Brownie and Jerome were part of the original unit. Before moving on, we spent nearly a month helping clean up the hotel. Since then, we've had a number of guys come and go from the unit. Eventually, they all get to meet Marie, including you."

From the other room, the two men heard the ringing of a bell. Doc began to stand, saying, "Sounds as if Marie has our refreshments ready. Let's go get something to eat. We can talk about this more later, if you want?"

Before leaving the room, Ross asked, "Is Sarge Marie's boyfriend?"

Thinking about it for minute, Doc said, "No. Actually I think Marie is trying to be a friend to everyone."

Chapter 8

Relinquishing the arm of her latest dance partner, Marie twirled away and stood in the middle of the ballroom, her arms extended out, hands raised in a grand gesture of welcome. Over the waltz music playing on the phonograph, she said to the gathered men around the room, "I trust today's entertainment has been to your enjoyment, but regretfully they must end."

The men sighed and moaned, but then collectively gave Marie a round of applause, to which she bowed and said, "Merci beau coup. Je suis desole. I am sorry, but I am told we must call it a night. Your sergeant here tells me, he and I have something important to discuss privately, and I certainly would not want to disappoint him. No?"

The men laughed and tossed out some playful jibes to Sarge. They of course, all knew what the discussion was about, but they also remembered Sarge's instructions to go along with his plans and to not make Marie suspicious. Marie and Sarge spending time alone during a visit, was nothing new. In fact, quite a few of the men had private "conversations" with Marie.

Marie continued addressing the group, "Except for Monsieur Cowboy, who I will definitely have to get to know better..." A quick round of ribbing of an embarrassed Private Ross interrupted Marie's speech temporarily, as she continued, "...you all know the rules. Feel free to select any of the rooms in the hotel. Feel free to take a bath. In fact, some of you could use one."

The men thanked Marie for her hospitality and each slowly started down the hall or up the stairs to find a room to sleep. As they filed off, leaving Marie and Sarge alone in the ballroom, she playfully called after them, "Be sure to leave your doors unlocked. I may have to check in on some of you tonight."

Sarge pulled out a cigarette and offered it to Marie, who politely refused. Not wanting to let it go to waste, he placed it in his lips, lit it with his Zippo, and took a deep drag of the tobacco. Exhaling the smoke in a long, controlled, self-satisfying breath, he walked over to one of the sofas and sat down. Looking back at Marie, he patted the empty space on the sofa with his hand, and gestured for her to follow.

Marie hesitated for a moment, licked her lips and pulled her hair back across her head. She slowly glided up to Sarge, standing directly in front of him. There were few lights on in the room, and Sarge noticed the way the moonlight streaming in through the window softly lit Marie's lithe body. She gave her shoulder length hair a final head-toss and gently whispered, "Mon ami, you did not have to go through such a production to be alone with me."

Sarge took another long drag on his cigarette and without turning his head, shaped his lips to blow the smoke to the side as to not hinder his view of Marie. He took her hand and pulled her down to sit beside him on the sofa. "I've got some important things to discuss with you."

Marie gracefully sat down and in the same fluid motion her left hand swept behind Sarge's back and settled gently, caressing the base of his neck. Sarge stiffened slightly at her touch and the fact she leaned forward, almost into his lap, her lips less than an inch from his. Softly gazing into Sarge's eyes, Marie asked, "Do we really have to talk about anything? Can't we just do what we both want?"

"You know what I want?"

Using her right hand to slightly open her blouse to expose a teasing glimpse of her full and ample bosom, she ran her finger through the valley between her breasts and said, "You know what I want. What more matters? No?"

Gently pulling her hand off of his neck, Sarge said, "Why do we always have to go through this?"

Returning her hand to its original position, Marie cooed into Sarge's ear, "I just keep hoping you'll change your mind."

Sarge's ire increased. He pulled both of Marie's hands away from himself and pushed her back. She huffed back on the sofa, a disappointed scowl on her face. Sarge said, "You know how I feel about you and what happened between us."

Marie pulled her skirt up over her knees and crossed her legs in a suggestive manner. Her response had a sharp edge to it when she said, "Would you rather I visited some of the other rooms? Do you like that better?"

Sarge pulled her skirt down, saying, "You know I don't like any of this. What you do when I'm not here, is your business. You can not blackmail me into bed."

"Do you not find me attractive?"

"You know how beautiful I think you are. It's just you and I have shared so much. I think of you as a sister, a little sister I need to protect. Now, can we drop this little game and talk about something else?"

"You do know your men think we are lovers, don't you?"

"They can think whatever they want. It's what I know that's important to me."

Realizing her pursuit had reached a dead end, Marie asked, "So, what is it which is so important you drove all the way out here? And why did you not come alone?"

Still trying to figure out how to explain his predicament without giving too much away, Sarge stammered out, "You're still pretty well connected with the, uh, you know, uh, high society types, aren't you?"

"The Germans changed a lot of things. Many people, like my father are dead. Depending upon how many of them are still alive, oui, I know a few. Why?"

Sarge finally got an idea when he said, "Well, I've got this friend whose mother died and left him all of this fancy jewelry. He's supposed to divide it up between all of the brothers and sisters."

"So why doesn't he just give a few to each?"

Improvising as he went, Sarge said, "Well, he thought of that, but he doesn't think he can divide them up evenly and he doesn't want any of the kids to feel cheated. Besides, a couple of the pieces have very large diamonds and stuff."

"I guess I don't see where I, how do you say it, fit in."

"This buddy of mine is thinking he could sell all of the jewelry and then divide the money. He is even thinking about taking the jewels out and melting down the gold, and selling them that way."

"It sounds like a good plan to me."

"Yeah, it did to me too, but there's a problem."

"What is this problem, mon ami?"

"Some of the pieces are quite rare and he's afraid a jeweler would recognize them, ask all kinds of questions and cause problems."

"Why would it be a problem? What questions could he ask?"

Sarge was stumped by this last question. He thought about it for a second and then modified his story with, "Well, my friend's mother was married to a jewel thief, and he's afraid some of his mother's jewels were once stolen. He's afraid some jeweler would recognize them and turn them into the police and then he'd never see them again."

"So, what is it this friend of yours needs to ask of me?"

"We, uh oops, I mean he was wondering if you knew someone who could give him an opinion as to the jewels' worth and what he should do with them, without calling the police or anyone."

With a knowing smile on her face, Marie thought for a moment and then said, "This is an interesting problem your friend has. I will have to think about this one for a while. You are staying for a few days. Let me think about it tonight and I'll give you an answer in the morning. Will your friend wait that long?"

Sarge wasn't sure how much he had given away with his slip of the tongue, but he was sure she knew his story was a deception. On the other hand, he figured if she was going to go along with it, he would too. So he told her, "Yeah. The morning would be fine. There's no hurry at all."

Marie stood and began to glide out of the room. She spoke over her shoulder, "Well, if you are not going to keep me company upstairs, I guess I'll just go to sleep by myself."

Chapter 9

After so many nights in the field, sleeping on the hard ground, the feather mattress of the bed felt good against Professor's back. The soft cotton sheets were such a contrast to the scratchy wool blanket he normally had for comfort. The friendly glow and toasty warmth of the fireplace served as a generous replacement for the cold damp morning air he fought the morning before.

All of these creature comforts deepened his sleep and lowered his sensitivity to the world around him. Professor did not hear the bedroom door's knob turn and slowly open. He did not hear the delicate bare feet glide across the wooden floor to the side of his bed. He did not feel the covers lift slightly from his body. He felt and sensed nothing until Marie's soft naked body slid into his bed.

If the silky heat of her body hadn't been enough to wake him, her whispered breath in his ear certainly was. “May I sweeten your dreams, mon ami?”

Without thinking, Professor rolled onto his side to face her. His right arm was already under her, held down at the elbow by Marie's waist. Without freeing it, he raised his forearm to support her back as he repositioned himself. Walter placed his left hand on her shoulder and began to pull Marie toward him. He stopped when their lips were less than an inch away and said, “If you are a dream, don't wake me.”

He pulled her tight to his chest, his dog-tags nestling themselves into the valley formed by her breasts. They kissed longingly, slow and deep, and then he pushed Marie away slightly. In the embrace, he had been able to raise his lower arm a bit and he used it to pull back her arm gently, until it was slightly behind her back.

Lying on her side, both arms under his control, Professor had the advantage of a free hand. Marie trembled slightly, but did not fear what he would do. Her breath quickened a bit when she said, "I appear to be at your mercy, monsieur."

Placing his index and middle fingers gently over her lips to quiet her, he asked, "Are dreams supposed to talk so much?"

Professor lowered his hand to her shoulder and then gently caressed the side of her breast with his fingers, his thumb nestled in the fold underneath. Marie stiffened and sighed at his touch. He barely touched her breast, cradling and lifting it slightly, but it was enough to arouse her desires.

Slowly he pulled the sheets back so he could see her naked silhouette against the glow of the fireplace. Professor returned his hand to her rib cage, but this time he turned it over so the back of his fingers and nails could follow the curves of her body.

He quietly traced a path down the slope of her waist and then back up the rising curve of her hip. When he reached the length of his reach, he made a U-turn on her thigh, pausing and hovering within the tops of the tufts of her pubic hair. Professor's fingers were touching only the barest tips of her hair, but he could feel the warm dampness below.

Marie tensed and quivered when his fingers brushed her bushy mound, but refrained from thrusting forward. She hungered for him to probe deeper, almost as much as she enjoyed the teasing, so she left the next move to him.

Professor changed direction and reached his fingers into the waistband of his underwear, quickly pulling them down and off his body. Tossing them into the darkness, he reached back to Marie's leg, taking the full back of her thigh, firmly in the grasp of his large hands. As he pulled Marie's pelvis up against his, Professor released Marie's arm and she threw it around his chest and they embraced tightly and intensely.

The intensity of their kissing increased, fueled by the puffing hot air pouring from each other's noses like charging bulls. The desperation of their embrace deepened, heightened by the sweat forming within and lubricating the spaces between their bodies.

Professor slid his hand up the back of Marie's thigh and cupped one cheek of her tight buttocks roughly in his hand, pulling her to him in a desperate but impossible attempt for them to be closer. As he pulled at her cute bottom, the gap between her thighs widened and his rising manhood popped into and filled the moist space.

Even though they were not yet joined, the added warmth and wetness on his penis caused Professor to break off his kissing and gasp for air. When he suddenly and surprising came into contact with her musky scented pubic lips, Marie had a similar but more spastic reaction as she rolled her eyes and plead, “Please don't stop now.”

Not that any encouragement was necessary, but Marie's request threw Professor into the throes of his full rutting glory. The long period of time in the field left him no more patience and he rolled onto his back pulling Marie along with and atop him. Her thighs eagerly and automatically parted to make room for his entry.

Professor grabbed Marie's waist in his hands and pulled her up and onto his member. She was wet and ready, but he gruffly pulled her down, his size and fervor causing her to gasp in momentary pain.

Now safely oriented on top of him, Marie threw her body back to a sitting position, her long dark hair flying backward in a long arc. His hands still held her hips at the waist and she used the leverage of placing her hands back onto his knees to further thrust her hips forward, desperately taking in as much of his manhood as she could.

The glowing fireplace softly lit their bodies. Marie rode Professor like an experienced cowboy on a bucking bronco. The same long period in the field which filled him with desire, deprived him of the control necessary to prolong the experience and in a few minutes he could not hold back the flooding contractions as he reached climax.

In one movement, Marie rode out the final thrusts and threw herself forward onto Professor, locking her legs around his, throwing her arms around his neck, and kissing him deeply until he couldn't breath. Rolling over with Marie still clinging desperately to him, Professor gasped for air and then slumped in a much relieved exhaustion.

Releasing her grip on Professor, Marie fell back, letting her arm drape gracefully over the edge of the bed. She took a few slow, deep breaths and then said, “I feel so much better now. You were tres magnifique.”

Coming down from his passion induced high, he realized fully for the first time who was in bed with him. Sobering up a bit, he asked, “Does Sarge know you are here?”

Crossing her arms slightly and pouting, she replied, “Let's not talk about him. Sarge would have me live the life of a nun.” Striking a more seductive pose, she continued, “Besides, I do not have the body of a nun. No?”

Rolling over toward her, Professor had to admit, “No, you do not look like a nun.”

“Did you not enjoy the fact I do not behave as a nun?”

Smiling and laughing, Professor kissed Marie and said, "Yeah, I have to admit your behavior disqualifies you to be a nun."

The two hugged and reflected in the afterglow of the moment, until Marie initiated her plan by whispering nonchalantly, "You must be feeling excited about your new found riches."

Trying to hide a surprised reaction and a shaky voice, he said, "I don't know what you're talking about."

"You don't have to hide the secret any longer. Sarge told me all about the jewels and the problems you are having in deciding how to divide them."

Now in a more relieved voice, Professor said, "Yeah. I've never seen anything like it. We've all been arguing about what to do with it, ever since we first found it. Finally, we all decided that if anyone would know what to do, you might."

"Sarge fell asleep in the middle of telling me how you found it."

"Actually it was Moocher who found it in the bottom of the wagon. He thinks he should get to keep it."

Trying to keep up her deception, Marie paused for a second to reconsider what she'd learned and plan what to ask next. She ran a finger through Professor's chest hairs and cooed, "Sarge does not have your stamina, cherie. He fell asleep just after saying you had found some jewels. You will have to finish his story about how you found them."

"We were cleaning up the town when I first spotted them pulling the wagon. That's why I think I have a better claim than Moocher. Anyway, there was something fishy about them three guys, so we checked it out. Turned out the three men were SS thugs trying to sneak out of town with a wagon full of stuff."

"Oh my, that must have been scary," squealed Marie.

"Yeah it was. We had to kill the three krauts. We didn't want to, but it's the way it all had to happen, I guess."

Coldly, Marie said, "No one is going to cry over the loss of a few Germans."

"Yeah. I suppose so. When we searched the wagon, Moocher found this ornately decorated wooden box. When we opened it, there it was. That's all there is to it."

Marie puzzled over how to get the rest of the answers to the questions in her mind. Eventually, she asked, "All Sarge could talk about were the jewels. I really won't be able to be of much help until I know exactly what it is. Can you give me a better description?"

"Sure I can. It is a heavy, possibly solid gold drinking chalice. Almost the entire surface is covered in large diamonds, rubies, and emeralds."

Excitedly, Marie sat up, pulling the sheets up to cover her breasts in a long past need for modesty. "Mon Dieu! Can it be possible?"

Surprised by her reaction, Professor asked, "What's the matter? It's just a hunk of gold with jewels. Personally, I say we melt it down and sell off the jewels."

Excited, but in a whisper, she said, "No. My God, no. You can't do that."

"Why not? What in the hell has you so spooked?"

Calming herself, she asked, "Are you familiar with the legend of King Arthur and the knights of the round table?"

"Of course I am. Why?"

"According to the legend, Arthur was afraid of petty quarreling among the knights and sought a common quest to bind their allegiance."

"Yeah. Yeah. I know about it. He told them God had commanded them to search out the Holy Grail. Are you saying this is the Grail?"

"No. It is not the Grail."

"I should say not, " he said pompously. "If anyone truly had the Grail, the world would certainly know where it was."

"Oui. I know this too, but there is more to the legend. It was said King Arthur sought a symbol to inspire the knights in their quest. So, he had a golden chalice created. Inset on the chalice were the finest gems in the realm. Does this sound familiar?"

"I hear what you are saying, but I don't ever remember reading any of this in books."

"Well, I suppose there are many versions to legends and many details which do not find their way into books."

Interested and amused, Professor asked, "Let's say you're right about this chalice. How did it get here and how did those SS thugs get it?"

"King Arthur's court was based upon law and the code of chivalry among the knights. Any dispute between knights would be brought to the king for judgment. When King Arthur would render his verdict, the two disputing parties would drink from this cup, signifying their respect for the law and the king. It was called the "Calice de Justice", the cup of justice."

"That explains what it is, but how did it get to France?"

"It is said that when Lancelot ran off to France with Guinevere. King Arthur and his knights chased him down to get her back. Some of the versions say during this campaign, King Arthur dies at the hands of his evil nephew Mordred. Arthur would surely have brought the cup with him to France."

"So you are saying it was lost in the battle?"

"As a little girl, I would sometimes hear visitors talk of the chalice, claiming it existed. They also claimed to know someone, who knew someone, who knew who owned it. We all thought them to be wild stories, but it seems they were true."

The logic of her story sunk in to Professor's mind and the profundity of the situation was not lost on him. "Oh my God," he spoke. "I can see now why we can't simply melt it down. As jewels and gold it may be worth a fortune, but as the Calice de Justice, it is priceless."

"What is it you will all do now?"

Yawning from post sex fatigue, he replied, "I don't know what we are going to do, but I am going to try and sleep on it. I'll deal with this in the morning. Would you like to stay here with me?"

Thinking about it a bit, Marie reached behind his head, cradling his neck and said, "No, mon cheri. I think I need to be alone right now."

Chapter 10

The door to Professor's bedroom burst open and almost simultaneously slammed shut. He woke thinking he was back in a foxhole and incoming artillery rounds were exploding all around him. His delusion wasn't far from the truth, except the explosions were Sarge.

"Who in the hell do you think you are?" screamed Sarge, pulling the Professor up by the neck.

Trying to focus his now bulging eyeballs, Corporal Bambridge struggled to breathe, forcing out, "What are you talking about?"

"You told her. Didn't you?" demanded Sarge without loosening his deadly grip.

Bambridge cuffed Sarge about the ears with his fists, breaking the hold on his airway. The release of tension caused him to roll out of the bed's other side and onto the floor. Keeping the bed between himself and Sarge, he struggled to his feet and yelled back, "What in the hell are you talking about?"

Recovering himself to a standing position, Sarge reorganized his shambled uniform, pointed an accusatory finger at Professor and hissed, "You told Marie about the chalice, you stupid son of a bitch. Didn't you?"

"I only filled in the holes she said you left out."

Relaxing a bit and softening his threatening pose, Sarge asked, "What are you talking about?"

"Marie came in here last night and said you'd already told her about the jewels. She said you fell asleep on her before you could tell her how we found them. I just filled in the blanks you left out."

Sarge looked skyward and slapped his hand of his forehead in a gesture of both disgust and embarrassment. He sat down on the edge of one of the side chairs and said, "That sneaky little bitch."

Puzzled, Bambridge lowered his guard and slowly sat on the edge of the mattress. "What are you getting at Sarge?"

"She tricked you," Sarge chuckled. "That sly little minx, tricked you."

"What?"

"After you all left the ballroom last night, I told her some friend of mine had inherited a bunch of jewels from his dead mother, and asked if Marie could help us sell them discreetly. She must not have bought my story."

Bambridge slapped his forehead and then sighed, "So Marie came in here and congratulated me on coming into some jewels, and tricked me into spilling my guts."

"How could you be so stupid?"

"What else can I say? I'm sorry, Sarge."

Thinking it over a bit, and waving his hand in a gesture of surrender, he said, "Hey, what's done is done. I'm sure we're not the first men she's tricked into playing the fool."

"And probably not the last." Both men sat for a moment shaking their heads, before something popped into Bambridge's mind and he asked, "What did she do? Come straight to you with it this morning?"

"She sure as hell did."

"What did she say?"

"She barged in on me while I was shaving and she was pretty pissed off," said Sarge. "She said she'd never let anyone melt down a treasure like King Arthur's cup, or something like it, and then stormed back out of the room. I figured only you could have come up with the King Arthur stuff."

"No Sarge. Marie figured that one out on her own. I just described the chalice to her. She seems pretty sure of her opinion." Professor thought about it for a moment and then stated, "I've got a better question. What are we going to do now?"

"Hell, this doesn't change anything. She knows what it is now. That's all. We figured we'd have to show it to her eventually."

"That's not the point now is it?"

Sarge asked, "What do you mean?"

"If Marie was as upset about it as you say, do you think she'll turn us in to some official person, or the police?"

Sarge thought it over for a minute, apparently changed his opinion a few times, and then said, "No. I don't think she'll do anything crazy. On the other hand, I don't think we need to take any chances. You go round up the men and meet me in the ballroom. I'll go find Marie and meet you there in ten minutes. We'll settle this thing, once and for all."

"Sounds good to me. I'll see you downstairs."

They headed for the doorway. Both stopped dead in their tracks when Professor desperately pulled on Sarge's shoulder. He asked, "Hey, Sarge. You don't think she'd grab the cup and run, do you?"

"Don't worry about it. After she yelled at me, it was the first thing I thought of. I know where the box is and it's safe. Now let's go."

Chapter 11

The men were already assembled in the ballroom when Sarge arrived with two packages in his arms. The first he carried in the crook of his elbow, the familiar brown wooden box containing the chalice. The second he carried by the crook of her elbow, the familiar figure of Marie.

Sarge released his grip on Marie to let her go off to wherever she might want to sit. Instead, she elected to remain standing. She crossed her arms and huffed, "I at least want to see it before I agree to help."

He found an appropriately small table and dragged it to the center of the room, placing the chest on top for all to see. Sarge opened the chest and pulled out the velvet bag shrouding the cup. He set it down and then slowly lowered the bag around the treasure.

The group could not help letting out sighs of admiration and awe as the morning sunlight glinted from the gold and jewels. The men felt compelled to raise their hands to shade their eyes, the image being so intense.

Marie fell to her knees and made the sign of the cross in reverence to the object.

"Well Marie," asked Sarge, "is it everything you thought it would be?"

"Certainement! From all I've heard as a child, this must be the Calice de Justice, King Arthur's Cup of Justice."

Moocher was the first to react to Marie's assertion. "You really know what this thing is?"

"Oui. At least as sure as I can be."

"What is she talking about Sarge?" asked Red.

Sarge didn't know the whole story, so he deferred to Marie, and asked, "Do you want to tell them, or would you rather have the Professor explain it?"

"Hey, what gives, Professor. Have you been holding out on us?" asked Carletti in a suspicious tone.

The Professor challenged back, "Have you got a problem, Fingers?"

A couple of the other suspicious men stood and Brownie demanded, "Did you know all along what this thing was?"

Marie jumped in to calm the rising tension with, "Professor did not know until I told him."

There was a moment for a round of tense stares before Tinker inquired, "So, Marie, what is this cup of justice?"

Marie told the story of King Arthur, Lancelot, and Guinevere, finishing up with, "As a girl, I'd hear the stories about the Calice de Justice and how it came to France. Many of our guests would talk about it. It was rumored to belong to someone in this general area, but no one quite knew who. Like many rumors about treasure, the magnitude of the story and the size of the riches increases with every telling of the tale. In this case, the actual chalice is far more wonderful than the stories."

Doc's southern accent cut in with, "Well if that don't put the chiggers on the hound dog."

Everyone turned and looked at him. Finally, Private Johnson asked, "What in the heck do you mean by it?"

"Chiggers are little lice-like creatures. They live in the grass and get on your skin, causing a rash and making you itch."

Red re-asked his question with, "I know what chiggers are. I want to know what the hell you meant by it?"

Doc finally realized his use of an obscure expression needed an explanation. He said, "Basically it means we're screwed. You can't take an itchy hound dog hunting and we sure as hell can't sell this thing outright if everyone will recognize what it is."

Brownie agreed. "The man's got a point. If it is that famous, there ain't no one going to be willing to buy it."

"Besides, some government official could claim it's a French art treasure and take it away from us," added Tinker.

Sarge took over the conversation, "Okay. We all know this. We've been down this road before. The question is, what do we do with it now?"

Brownie stood and somewhat angrily said, "I've been saying since the beginning, we pry the jewels off, melt down the gold, and divide it up as best we can."

"I will not allow you to destroy the chalice," said Marie defiantly. "To destroy such a beautiful work of art in the name of greed is crazy. The chalice has survived for hundreds of years and now you want to chop it up. You should be ashamed of yourselves."

Many of the men did feel the shame. Many were simply bystanders waiting for the group to decide. Some were still gripped by greed. Carletti was one of the latter. "Who cares. We can't sell it intact. We can't give it to just one of us. I say we melt it down."

Jerome suggested, "Uh, no offense, but I would be willing to take it off all of your hands. I can appreciate its beauty and respect its history."

"Bullshit, Jerome," hissed Carletti. "You're a Jew. All you respect is the money you can get for it."

"Eat me, Fingers!"

Carletti jumped on the Jew, and the two wrestled on the floor until Sarge stepped in and pried the two apart. "Both of you, sit down and shut up. This pissing and moaning has been going on since we found the damned cup. Let's figure out what to do with it."

The Professor stood up and said, "Let's go through this thing logically. Let's look at our options and sort them out, one by one. Are we agreed?"

The men nodded and Sarge said, "You got the floor, Professor."

"Okay. Are we in agreement it would be nearly impossible to smuggle this thing home to the states?"

Sarge answered that one, "Yeah, I'd say so. They search our mail and packages. I've been told they're on the lookout for guys shipping things home, so even regular business shipments have been searched. We might be able to figure out a way, but the odds are, we'd get caught."

"Fine, so that option is gone. I think we are all in agreement, as well, we can not sell it around here."

"There ain't too many people with more than the shirt off their back," said Red.

Tinker added, "That thing's too famous anyway. One word leaking out and the French police would snap it up."

Professor thought for a second and then continued with, "I think we all agree there's no sense in turning it over to the Army."

A whole series of signals and gestures from the group made it obvious no one would stand for that option.

Brownie said, "Okay, so we're back to my idea. Let's break it up and melt it down."

Sarge turned to Marie and asked, "Are you still opposed to it?"

Marie calmly said, "Oui. I would give my life fighting to defend the chalice. It would be a sin to destroy it. If I hear you are going to break it up or melt it down, I will turn you all in to the Army as criminals." A few of the men agreed and sided with Marie.

In frustration and being facetious, Professor said, "Well I guess the only option left is for one of us to keep it. Do you want to draw straws for it?"

Brownie suggested, "I'll arm wrestle all of you for it."

"Let's draw numbers," said Red.

The suggestions grew in absurdity and tensions grew with each idea. Finally, the chaos increased until it was evident they would soon break out into fighting. Sarge stepped into the middle of the room and shouted, "That does it! We've been arguing about this ever since we found the damned thing and now we're back where we started. We can't unload it. We can't divide it up. And there's no way we can fairly decide which one person gets it."

The weight of desperation and futility fell upon the group, settling in as silence. Marie cut the silence with, "Maybe there is a way to resolve this matter."

Stunned, everyone sat down in their chairs and Sarge asked, "What are you talking about?"

"There is an old tradition within the banking community in France. It goes back hundreds of years, to before the French Revolution. When a number of men held a dispute over property or possessions, or families held joint claims to the estates of their fathers, the bank would create a tontine."

"What is a tontine?" asked Tinker.

"How should I say it? Well, the parties give the bank the money, or property to hold. All of the parties sign a contract which agrees the property goes to the last surviving person."

"You mean you have to die to collect?" asked a confused Red.

"No. Not at all. For you all, you take the box to a bank. The bank does not care what is in it. They put it in the vault and you all sign a document, the tontine. Then, many years from now, the last one of you alive, gets the chalice."

Tinker added his two cents. "You know, one really good thing about this is, whoever gets the chalice will be at retirement age and the money could let someone live a grand life. I think it's a great idea."

"It is unless Fingers, over there, gets his family to bump you all off," accused Jerome.

Chuckling, but not hostile, Carletti said, "You should worry Jerome, because if I do, I'll have them start with you."

Sarge took over the floor, saying, "Okay, so we're all in agreement. Tomorrow we'll load up the truck and drive into Paris, find the biggest bank we can, draw up this tontine thing, and unload this pain-in-the-ass cup once and for all. All in favor say aye."

The cheers made it clear everyone, although a bit unclear with the details, was happy with the decision.

Chapter 12

"Monsieur Cowboy. Is this seat taken?"

Surprised to see Marie, he stuttered a bit when he said, "Yes. I mean no. I mean, if you want to sit down, I can..."

"Pardon moi. I did not mean to startle you. May I sit next to you."

A bit relieved, Cowboy swallowed and eventually said, "Sure."

Gracefully taking her seat on the cast-iron garden bench. Marie pulled her shawl a bit tighter around her shoulders, and cozied up to Cowboy's shoulder which made him feel still more uncomfortable. "What are you doing out here by yourself?" she asked.

"I always seem to think better out of doors."

"Are you really a cowboy?"

"I don't know. I guess you could say so. My daddy owns a cattle ranch back in Oklahoma."

Marie snaked her arm through Cowboy's, gave a slight squeeze, and asked, "Do you ride a horse?"

"Oh, yeah, you pretty much have to. There ain't too many roads into them hills. Just about the only way to keep the cattle in control is from the back of a horse."

"I've seen a western movie. It seems so exciting. Riding the range. Fighting Indians and such."

Cowboy laughed and said, "There ain't no Indians. Well, at least none we have to fight."

"But, in the movie, the Indians are always attacking the cowboys. Is it not like that?"

"No. It's not. In fact, we have a few Indians working on the ranch."

Marie seemed a bit disappointed, but none the less, she continued her fantasy. "Do you carry a six-gun?"

"Some of us do. Some of us carry a rifle on our saddle. But, they ain't for shooting Indians."

"Why do you carry them?"

"Actually, most of the time we use them for shooting rattlesnakes. Once in a while, a coyote may wander into the herd and we'd have to shoot it. Sometimes, we'd have a steer get sickly or break a leg, and we'd have to shoot it to put it out of its misery."

"Did you ever have a shoot-out with a bad guy?"

Cowboy started to laugh and then fell into a shocked silence. His body tensed a bit and then went limp. Marie felt this sudden change of emotion and asked, "What's the matter? Did you kill the bad guy?"

Cowboy wiped his face, fighting back tears. "I never had a shoot-out back home. I had my shoot-out with those Germans, over that damned cup. I killed a man over a stinking cup."

Marie tried to soothe his nerves. "Do you want to tell me what happened?"

"Ain't much to say. The guy pulled a gun and pointed it at me. I didn't even think. I just pulled the trigger. Next thing I know, the guy's dead."

Marie squealed with delight and said, "You see? You really are a cowboy. The bad guy pulled his gun, but you were faster. You are a hero. You are my hero."

Marie turned him around and pulled his face to hers, planting a big kiss on his lips. Cowboy instantly forgot the horror of the shooting. It was replaced in his eyes by the terror of Marie's unexpected kiss. His eyes expanded to the size of dinner plates. Realizing she must have hit a sensitive nerve with the young man, she retreated behind a quick, "Pardon. I'm sorry. I got so excited. Can you forgive me?"

Regaining his composure, Cowboy said, "It's okay Ma'am. I just got caught by surprise."

"I don't know if I like you calling me ma'am. It makes me sound so old. Do I look old to you?"

Blushing a bit, he said, "No, Ma'am...I mean Miss. I think you're quite beautiful."

"Good," she said. "May I ask a favor of you?"

"Of course you can."

"Well, Monsieur Cowboy, I'm having a little bit of a problem with one of my horses. Would you mind going over to the barn with me and looking at her?"

"I'd be more than willing to look in on your ailing mare. You just lead the way."

Marie took Cowboy's arm and led him through the moonlit path toward the barn. She easily knew her way, but she was in no hurry, holding tightly to Cowboy as if she needed support. When she arrived at the barn, Marie opened the small door and struck a match to light the lantern mounted on the wall. The flash of light momentarily blinded Cowboy until his eyes adjusted to the warm, yellow glow of the lamplight.

Cowboy could see the entirety of the small barn. He saw hay piled loosely about the walls and floor. He saw harnesses, implements, and tools. He saw Marie's silhouette, cast by the lamp onto the wall, but he saw no horses. He sniffed the air and knew right away there hadn't been horses in this barn for some time.

"You tricked me into coming down here. You don't have any horses do you?"

Tossing her hair a bit, Marie said, "Yes, I tricked you, and no there are no horses."

"Why?"

Marie glided around to where Cowboy was somewhat between her and the lamp, letting the soft light caress her form and let him clearly see her. Marie loosened the shawl and let it fall partially off of her bare shoulders. The cotton, drawstring top of the peasant blouse she had on, did not completely cover her ample cleavage. She waited until Cowboy's gaze lifted and returned to her face before saying, “It was so chilly outside, but in here, it is warm and cozy. Don't you agree?”

The barn brought back pleasant memories for him and made him feel at ease, almost as if he were back home. He took in a deep breath and remembered the characteristic smell of drying hay. He sensed the humid, sort of fertile smell in the air. The obvious smell of cut grass, fermenting soil, and even a trace of the sweat spent in harvesting it.

There was warmth in the air, coming from the hay as it dried. Small bits of chaff floated on the currents rising and falling in front of the lamplight, and you could almost see the mixture of vapors rising from the piles. He stooped to pick up a few pieces, held them to his nose and said, “Yeah, this is nicer than outside. If it weren't for this uniform and you standing there, I'd say I was back in Oklahoma.”

Marie silently turned around and in a graceful swirl, she removed the shawl and spread it gently on the mattress of hay. She lowered herself onto the shawl, sitting as if she were posing like some Greek statue. She patted the ground next to her, beckoning the young man to sit next to her. "Come over here," she said softly. “Let's make believe this is Oklahoma.”

Reluctantly at first, Cowboy walked the short distance to her, momentarily looming over Marie as if he wasn't sure what to do next. She reached up and took his hand in hers, gently but with a purpose. “It's all right. You can trust me.”

He lowered himself to the floor and Marie gently directed him to lay down so his head was cradled in her lap. He was still tense, but Marie stroked his hair and hummed a soft tune. Slowly, Cowboy relaxed into Marie's control. In a few minutes, he was calm as a lamb relaxing at his mother's side.

"Does this feel more like home?" she asked.

"Home never felt like this."

Still stroking his hair, twirling small locks of it around her finger, Marie asked, "Do you have a girlfriend at home?"

"No. Out on the ranch, there weren't many women around, and we were too busy to think much about it."

"Is there not some local girl who has caught your eye? Some one who makes your heart go, how do you say, pitter-patter?"

Cowboy thought idly for moment and then quietly said, "Nope."

Leaning forward so her breasts pressed against his cheek, she whispered in his ear, "So, you've never been with a woman?"

"No Ma'am."

Marie slid a hand down the open collar of his shirt, which caused him to tremble slightly. Then she grabbed what little chest hair he had and painfully pulled on it saying, "If you call me ma'am one more time, I will leave. Call me Marie, cheri, or anything else but ma'am."

Marie released his hair and lowered her lips to his before he could answer. She kissed him long and slow, until she felt him responding. She could feel his mood shift. His hormones were awakening. His fear was replaced by passion. The lamb was gone, replaced by a young bull.

He clumsily grabbed for her blouse and brusquely pawed a breast. She grabbed his hand and whispered into his ear, "Let me do the work. Trust me and follow my lead. You just relax and enjoy it. Do you trust me?" Cowboy nodded and she kissed his cheek.

Marie slipped out from under him and lowered him back to the floor. Sitting beside and facing him, she unbuttoned his overshirt and pulled the tails out of his waistband. She placed her fingers on his flat stomach and slid them slowly up his chest. By the time she reached his face, Cowboy's back was arching and his eyes had rolled back in his head. As she lifted the touch of her hands, he relaxed and began to breathe again.

She sat back, casually untied the drawstring, and pulled the top of the peasant blouse down to her waist. Cowboy swallowed gamely as her breasts popped out for view. She removed her arms from the sleeves and returned her hands to the belt of his pants. Releasing the pressure on the canvas belt, sliding the brass buckle's catch out of the way, she pulled the excess tail of the belt free.

Unbuttoning his pants, she fished out the tail of his undershirt with a fingernail. The other nine quickly found their way around his waist under the hem of the shirt and started to slide along his belly taking the shirt up with them.

As she neared his chest, her nipples danced across his navel and ultimately the warmth of her breasts came into full contact with the sweat beading on his chest. Without thinking, Cowboy wrapped his arms around her and held her tight. Marie used his grasp to pull him slightly upright and released enough of the embrace to slide both shirts off of him.

Letting him fall back onto the hay, she sat back and tended to the pants which by now were under maximum tension. She unzipped his fly and pulled both the waistband of his pants and his boxer shorts down off of his hips. With the khaki material removed, the remaining tent pole stood naked in the lamplight.

Marie stood up and reached under her skirt with one hand, deftly pulling off her panties, tossing them to where his shirts were watching the proceedings. She stepped over him with one leg, letting the hem of her skirt drape around his hips as she straddled over him. She spread out the long skirt, almost covering his entire body as she lowered herself upon him.

She carefully positioned herself so he could feel the warmth between her legs, but she did not allow him inside her. Because Marie knew he'd need time to adjust to the sensations flooding his body right now, she pulled some of the skirt off of his chest and lowered herself down in a long bare-chested hug.

Marie could feel his hot breath coming in quick huffs against her neck. She waited for the spastic breaths to smooth out and lengthen a bit before whispering to him, "Are you okay, my love?"

"I'm not sure," he trembled out.

"Just relax," she cooed. "I will not hurt you. You have nothing to prove to me. Allow me to pleasure you. Trust me and everything will be wonderful."

She sat up and lifted herself slightly from his body. Reaching under her skirt, Marie gently took him in her hand and quietly directed him into her. Marie brushed the head of his penis across her pubic hair, allowing some of the lubricating wetness to coat him. Slowly she lowered herself around him, pausing each moment she felt he was going to lose control.

Finally, he was completely inside of her and she lowered herself to his chest. Without moving her hips at all, she hugged his tense body until she could feel him adjust to the intensity. From this position Marie felt she could best monitor his reactions. "Hug me. Kiss me," she begged.

When she knew he was concentrating on the embrace, Marie started to slide her hips slightly in a gentle rocking motion, slowly at first, each stroke getting longer until she could safely slide along the entire length of his shaft. Each time she felt him nearing climax, Marie slowed and pinched his nipple to take his mind away from the stimulation.

Marie asked, “Are you enjoying this?” Cowboy was too busy to offer more than an unintelligible moan.

Marie quickened the pace of her stroking and could begin to feel the release building inside of him. Like a rodeo rider, she sat upright and squeezed her vaginal muscles to more tightly hold on to the saddle.

In response to the added stimulation, Cowboy's neck tendons tightened and his breathing came in rapid snorts through his nose. Suddenly, he let out a roar, throwing his head back in spasm. He arched his back wildly into the air, lifting Marie in the air. Like an expert rider, she swayed back and forth, in rhythm, remaining firmly seated upon her mount.

As Cowboy fell back exhausted, Marie deftly swung one leg over his body and slid off this spent bucking bronco, and laid next to him, waiting for him to recover. Cowboy reached out for her hand and clung to it desperately. Still panting a bit, he said, “I never thought it would feel so good.”

“I am glad you enjoyed yourself. For me, it was a great pleasure as well. You truly are a cowboy, so strong and virile.”

“That's kind of you to say, ma...I mean Marie. I know I will never forget this. I wish there was more I could do for you.”

Smiling out of Cowboy's sight, Marie's plan had worked. With a twinkle in her eye, she said, “There is one tiny favor you could do for me, my love.”

"Whatever it is, you name it, and I'll do it."

"Tomorrow when all of you go to Paris to make the tontine, please make sure my name gets added to the list."

"Gee, I don't know if I can do that."

"You will not be my hero?"

Cowboy felt obligated as he said, "I certainly would like to help you, but I'm worried about the other guys. I don't know what they'd say. I'd have to have some reason to include you."

Pouting, she said, "After all, it was I who told you what it was and where to go for the tontine. I think it is not asking too much to be included in the contract."

Rolling over to face her, Cowboy took her hand in his and pledged, "I don't know if I can get them to add your name, but if I am the one who gets the chalice, I promise you I will come back and share the wealth with you."

Chapter 13

1965

The banner above the doorway read, "20th Anniversary, Here's To Your Health Club". The small ballroom, in a hotel, outside O'Hare airport in Chicago was set up for a dinner party of ten.

One large round table waited in the middle of the room. It was illuminated by the low hanging crystal chandelier. It was set with china and crystal reflecting the light, waiting to receive its guests and cuisine.

In the front of the room was a lectern and microphone, flanked by the American flag on one side and an Army flag on the other. A tall stool, draped with a small tablecloth, stood beside the lectern. Atop the stool was a filled water pitcher and two glasses.

The only other furniture in the room, set in one corner. It was a small portable bar, stocked and ready for service, and manned by a lone bartender. He stood as the only sentry, awaiting the arrival of the guests.

Through the open doorway strode a one-armed man, the left sleeve of his suit jacket carefully folded and pinned to a tasteful length, fitting the remaining portion of his upper arm. He confidently walked up to the bartender.

As he came into the light from the back-lit doorway, the bartender could see the man was wearing an Army hat, and he could clearly see the gold chevrons pinned on it. The barkeep asked, "What'll you have to drink sergeant?"

Sarge reached into his pocket and pulled out a pack of cigarettes. "Scotch. Neat," he said.

While his drink was being poured, Sarge deftly shook the pack until one cigarette extended far enough to get his lips on it. He pulled the butt out and slipped the pack back into his coat pocket, his hand returning with the ever trusty Zippo in it. With practiced hand, Sarge flipped the lid and was ready to spin the flint wheel, when a hand shot forward holding a lighter. A voice attached to the hand said, "Let me get it for you."

Sarge lit the cigarette and removed it from his mouth as he turned to see who had offered the light. "Doc! Great to see you."

Sarge reflexively reached out his right hand, filled with the Zippo and a lit cigarette, to shake Doc's hand. Their hands met in a awkward manner and then they thought better and lowered them. Doc offered, "Sorry to hear about the arm."

Looking down to where his left arm should be, Sarge replied, "Yeah. Damned accident on the docks. Stupid kid working the crane swung some big crate against it. Could have been worse. Another foot and he'd have gotten me across my chest."

"Well, sorry about it anyway."

"Thanks."

Having overheard his nickname, the bartender asked, "What can I get for you, Doc?"

"Just some white wine, please."

Walter Bambridge had come up along side of them as they were speaking and piped in with, "Sounds like a typical California kind of drink order."

"Professor," chimed Sarge and Doc in unison.

"I hear it really is professor now. Is it true?" asked Doc.

"Sure is. I'm a professor in the Physics department at Northwestern University in Chicago."

Putting his cigarette in his mouth, Sarge extended his hand, shook Walter's and said, "Congratulations. I always knew you'd become an egghead."

The three men stopped their conversation for moment when they heard a familiar voice ask the bartender for a beer. Sarge tipped his glass toward him and said to the bartender, "That boy looks too young to be drinking. I'd check for some identification."

"Screw you guys," quipped Red.

Another new voice joined the group. It was Moocher who said, "Jesus, Red. You still look like your nineteen. When are you going to grow up?"

"I'll grow up when you get some hair, Moocher."

Doc came over and shook Moocher's hand. "Great to see you again. We Southern California guys will have to stick together."

"Always did. Didn't we?"

Sarge asked them, "What are you talking about?"

"About the time I was finishing medical school, Moocher was opening a pawn shop. I was always hard up for money and Moocher helped me out."

"Yeah and you paid me back every penny. Ain't too many people who do that."

Everyone stopped talking, when a voice from the doorway cried out, "Yoo-hoo. Hey fellas, lookie who I found in the hallway."

It was Tinker, dressed in a manner which would best be described as flamboyant. He had his arm around the shoulder of an embarrassed and uncooperative Anthony Carletti.

Fingers was dressed impeccably. His suit was expensive and custom tailored. He had a silk handkerchief peeking out from his pocket and a red carnation was in his lapel. He pulled Tinker's arms off his shoulder, dusted himself off, walked toward the bar and said, "That guy hasn't changed a bit. If anything, he's worse. I need a drink!"

Everyone chuckled and the attention suited Tinker just fine. He glided across the floor as if dancing on air and then pretended to take a bow. He held a pair of opera glasses to his eyes and giggled out, "This is definitely my kind of party...all men!"

Tinker took another bow and started a little twirl, but as he started to spin, he ran into a mountain of a man. He backed off and noticed the boots, the hat, and realized who it had to be. He threw his arms around the man and said, "Cowboy. My, how you've grown up."

Sarge came over and peeled Tinker off Cowboy, shook his hand and said, "Damn if he isn't right. Last time I saw you, you were this little toothpick of a boy. What happened?"

"You know what they say. That war made boys into men. I got home and spurted up."

Moocher, who was barely five foot four, asked, "Just how big are you?"

A little bit embarrassed, Casey said, "I'm six foot four or so and weigh two hundred and thirty pounds."

A couple of the guys whistled at the answer. Red yelled from near the bar, "Let's get the big guy a beer."

The crowd of men continued to laugh and joke, reminiscing and catching up on the past. At one point, a small amount of applause began to break out as Jerome Miller entered the room. Once Sarge realized who had entered the room he raised his glass and said, "Let's hear it for our resident editor-in-chief and the keeper of the newsletter, Jerome."

The group of men cheered in unison, recognizing the contribution the Jew had made to their little gathering. As he passed through the group, on his way to the bar, Jerome received many handshakes of thanks. Carletti stopped him, shook his hand, and said, "Jerome. I know I gave you a lot of grief when you suggested this newsletter for keeping all of us in touch, but I've got to hand it to you, it works and it's even entertaining. You're doing a great job."

"I didn't know you could read," ribbed Jerome.

"Screw you. I was seriously trying to compliment you on the job you've done on the newsletter."

"Thanks. I never thought I'd hear you say something like that."

The congratulatory gathering stopped when there was a commotion at the doorway. Some cussing and swearing was coming from the hall. A security guard dragged in a struggling black man, whose style of dress was second only to Tinker's in outrageousness. The captive man asked the group, "Would one of guys please tell this son-of-a-bitch I belong here. I've been trying to get him to listen to me for the past ten minutes."

Sarge stepped forward, motioned for the guard to release Brownie, and asked him, "What's the matter, officer?"

Brownie didn't wait for the guard to answer. He straightened his wide-brimmed hat and dusted off the arms of his green velvet suit, saying, "This peckerhead's trying to call me a pimp."

The guard said, "Well, look at the way he's dressed."

Sarge took the guard out of the room, explaining the situation and allowing Brownie to vent to the men. "Damn dumb white guy. No offense guys. Tries to haul my butt off to jail because he thinks I'm a pimp. I've got half a mind to sue this hotel."

Sarge had returned by now and he said, "Brownie, it's great to see you, but if I'd seen you in the lobby dressed like this, I'd be reaching for my wallet and asking, 'How much' myself." Sarge broke out laughing and so did most of the other men.

Brownie thought for second and then got caught up in the humor. "Yeah, I guess he had a point." Laughing and straightening himself up a bit, he said, "But you have to admit. I was styling."

Laughter broke out and the revelry continued until a waiter stepped to the lectern and said, "Gentlemen. If you will take your seats, dinner will be served."

The men took their drinks and settled into their seats around the large round dinner table. Three waiters served the group somberly. The men chatted, but the boisterous atmosphere of earlier was slowly replaced by more ceremony and each began to deal with the real reason they were all here. Each had a chance to count their blessings at being here at all.

Shortly after dessert, the waiters brought in champagne buckets and placed them around the table. They removed the used plates, tidied the tables and then, according to Sarge's instructions, left the room. The head waiter went over to the doors and closed them, making sure they were locked against someone entering from outside.

The waiter looked around to ensure all tasks were finished and then walked over to Sarge. "Sir," he said. "The room is locked as you requested. If there is nothing else, we shall leave you alone."

"Thank you."

The waiter nodded, clicked his heels in salute and then headed for the kitchen door. Sarge waited until the waiter left the room and was sure no one would interrupt their gathering. Sarge stood and took a fork in his hand. Tapping the fork on a drinking glass to get everyone's attention, he said, "Gentlemen. Let us get down to business. Would someone please open the champagne?"

Three of the men volunteered, opening the bottles and one at a time filling their friends' glasses. Sarge took his filled glass up to the lectern and said, "Gentlemen, please rise."

The men stood in their places at the table and faced Sarge. Each raised their glass and waited. Sarge was stolid in his expression. He mechanically said, "It is my pleasure to salute each of you tonight. Twenty years have passed since our tour of duty ended in the war. It is slightly more than twenty years since we entered into our contract. I am pleased to see all ten of us are here. I thank God none of us was killed in the war. I thank God none of us has been felled by disease or injury. Gentlemen. I drink to your health."

"Here, here," said the group and they sipped their champagne and patted each other on the back. They began to sit, when Sarge cleared his throat and added, "I'd like to make another toast."

Everyone wondered what he was going to say. They could tell by Sarge's expression, it was serious. Sarge raised his glass again and said, "Two years ago, she passed away. Although she was not officially one of our group, she was. Without her, we may have chosen to do something far worse than we did. She was a friend and we miss her. Gentlemen, I drink to Marie."

"Marie," sighed the group and they sipped their champagne. All of the men took their seats except for Sarge, who had business to tend to. He shuffled some papers on the lectern, which wasn't exactly easy for a man with one hand.

Sarge looked up at the group and said, "I'll keep this brief. First, I'd like to once again thank Jerome. For the past twenty years he has been publishing our twice-a-year newsletter, 'Here's To Your Health'." He let the applause subside before continuing, "Without it, I doubt this dinner would have taken place. We created the newsletter with the intent of letting us know when one of us died. It has turned out to be a vehicle of friendship and family."

Everyone nodded agreement and looked around the table at long-time friends. Friends who secretly hoped to be the last one left alive. Sarge continued, "I know some of you are wondering about the cup. As you know, Doc recently returned from Paris, where as part of his vacation, he was able to stop by and confirm everything is fine. The contract is still on file and the cup is still in the vault. Our tontine is still intact. Gentlemen, before we call this dinner to an end and continue our partying, I'd like to make one last toast. To the object of our meeting, the purpose of our agreement, the tie which binds us, let us drink a toast to the Calice de Justice."

The men stood as one, lifted their glasses, and chanted as one, "Calice de Justice." They drank until their glasses were empty and then threw them against the wall, breaking them in a shower of glass.

Chapter 14

Inspector Dunbar was sitting behind the wheel of his car, near Fisherman's Wharf, eating an Italian sausage sandwich from his favorite San Francisco street vendor, when he received the radio dispatch call. He looked over to his partner and said in an exasperated tone, "Ain't it always this way, Del? You just get relaxed and about the time you take the second bite of a glorious sandwich like this, some poor stiff's body gets found and we have to roll."

Inspector Delano Panetti, force-swallowed his food, wadded up the remainder in its waxed paper wrapper, and said, "You know, Josh, you take your food way too seriously. You've got to lighten up."

Josh Dunbar held up his remaining sandwich like a trophy, examining it, and said, "How can you say that? Look at this. It's a work of art. Now answer the call."

Inspector Panetti picked up the microphone of the radio and keyed it, "Inspector 27 responding. We'll be there in ten minutes." He pulled out a portable, red flashing light, placed its magnetically mounted base onto the roof of the car, and turned it on.

Rewrapping the rest of his sandwich, Inspector Dunbar started the car's engine, dropped it into gear, and headed out into traffic. "Did you get the address, Del?"

"Yep. Polk Street, just about even with Lombard. There's already a couple of patrol cars there, so I don't think we'll have trouble spotting it."

Josh turned left, heading south on Polk. Several blocks later they spotted the flashing lights of the police cars. Pulling up behind the last car, they were motioned through the gathering crowd by one of the officers on the scene. They parked the car, but before exiting the vehicle, Inspector Dunbar stuffed one last, huge bite of sandwich into his mouth. "No ufe wetting it go to maste," he mumbled out through a small spray of bread crumbs. His partner just shook his head and laughed.

Using the sleeve of his trench coat as a makeshift napkin, Josh wiped the bread crumbs and tomato sauce from his lips, and forced down the last of his sandwich. Holding his badge out to the first officer he met, he said, "Inspector Dunbar, homicide. This is Panetti. What have we got here?"

The officer replied, "I wasn't the responding officer. I'm just securing the crime scene, Inspector. All I know is we have one John Doe upstairs in the rear apartment."

Looking at the patrolman's name tag, Dunbar continued, "Okay, Officer Haase. Has the coroner arrived?"

"They've been called. You beat them here, but I suspect they'll be here any minute. The crime scene people were a little quicker. They're here and already upstairs."

"That's good. Thanks for your help."

Dunbar and Panetti walked around the front of the building, up the side alley, and walked through the door pointed out by another officer. They climbed the narrow stairs. The lighting was poor, intermittently contrasted by the light of camera flashbulbs coming from the open door at the top of the stairs. As his eyes reached the next floor's level, one of the flashes caused Delano to stumble and almost fall back onto Dunbar, who said, "Jesus, Del. You were just old and fat. Are you getting clumsy on me too?"

"You're no spring chicken yourself. If I fall, just make damned sure you catch me."

The two inspectors reached the apartment door and cautiously looked inside. They saw a rather large, by San Francisco standards, apartment. The walls were decorated with posters from movies and Broadway shows. The color scheme was the typical modern motif of lime greens, orange, and pinks. Colors flowed into each other and peace symbols were randomly on display. This was a decorative style the two officers had seen hundreds of times.

However, there were differences their trained police eyes captured and filed away for future use. The furniture wasn't the simple, utilitarian type they expected to see. The sofa was overstuffed, large, and frilly, almost Victorian. An ornately patterned, red silk kimono was thrown across one of the arms. There were floral scented candles burning in decorative glasses on the side tables.

Near the kitchen area was a small, equally ornate cafe table and two chairs. The remains of a take-out, Chinese dinner for two littered its surface. A purple fabric, swag lamp with fringed edges hovered over the table. A pink light bulb cast a strange hue over the chicken chow mein.

A sound, off to their right, caught their attention. One of the crime scene investigators emerged from the bedroom. The rattling of a hanging bead curtain which served as a door, took a few seconds to cease. Looking up, wiping his hands with a handkerchief, he said in a excited voice, "Hey Josh. Long time no see. I see you still got your shadow." Looking at Panetti and reaching out to shake his hand, he continued, "Good to see you, Del. How can you stand working with this guy?"

Inspector Dunbar laughed and patted the investigator on the back and quipped, "Lookie here. It's Bill. Someone must have left your cage door unlocked."

About the time this mutual admiration society meeting was getting started, the representative from the coroner's office arrived with his large black bag. Inspector Dunbar didn't recognize the technician, so he went over to introduce himself. "I'm afraid I don't recognize you. I'm Inspector Dunbar. This is my partner, Panetti. We're the Homicide team who's been assigned to the case. The tall one over there is Bill Jackson, one of the crime scene investigators. He's been here awhile, but my partner and I just got here, so your timing is perfect."

Putting the big bag down and removing his coat, the technician shook Josh's hand and said, "I'm Jeremy Williams. I just joined the San Francisco office, but I moved here from Chicago where I worked for five years. This is my first case here."

Bill Jackson reached for a glass in the drying rack on the countertop and filled the tumbler from the tap. "You're going to love this one, then," he said. He drank the water, wiped a drip from his lips, and shook his head before chuckling, "You're just going to love this one."

Dunbar turned around and snipped, "What in the hell are you talking about?"

Instead of answering, Bill put a smug grin on his face and walked over to the doorway. He carefully pulled the multi-colored beads, hanging in the entry, aside with his left hand. He took his right hand and bowing slightly at the waist, he gestured for the others to enter the room. Still chuckling, he said, "I'll just let you see for yourself."

The trio of investigators walked into the bedroom. Two other men who were industriously collecting evidence, stopped their efforts, seeming to wait to see the reaction on the new men's faces. The bedroom was something to behold. It looked more like a dressing room for an old-time movie star. A make-up table was on one wall, its huge mirror ringed with light bulbs.

There was a tri-fold screen in one corner, its top littered with draped clothing. Another corner was filled with a canopy bed, its fringed edge complimenting the pillows scattered across the quilt. In front of the closet was an overstuffed, oversized chair, its large footstool draped with the officers' object of interest, the victim.

Dunbar pointed to the victim and asked, "What the hell is this all about?"

Bill Jackson, who had quietly slid in behind the inspector, whispered in Josh's ear, "I told you you'd get a kick out of this."

The victim was naked. Posed almost like a statue, the male was draped, face down, over the hassock. The victim was kneeling, his thighs against the stool and his arms hanging on either side of the platform. His head wasn't buried in the padding as you would expect. Instead, it was raised, facing straight forward with a small apple stuffed in his mouth, like a roast pig. If the body were in full rigor mortis, you could pull the hassock out from under victim and it would probably stay there like a crawling child.

Walking around the body provided few clues. There were no unusual marks or bruises. As far as they could tell, there were no wounds, either by a gun or a knife. There was no large pool of blood. The only thing unusual was a small line of blood running from the victim's anus, down his thigh, forming a small puddle between the legs.

The coroner's technician set his black bag on the floor, opened the tacklebox-like lids, and started to examine the body. Inspector Dunbar looked up at Jackson, pointed at the body a second time and repeated, "What the hell is this all about?"

Jackson shrugged his shoulders, still grinning, saying, "Damned if I know."

Panetti chimed in, "Overdose of drugs?"

Jackson stated, "No drugs in the house. At least none we've found. No ligature marks. No signs of manual strangulation. I thought with the apple in his mouth, he may have smothered."

Dunbar started speculating, "Okay. We've got no bruises, no cuts, no stab wounds, and no gunshot wound..."

Jeremy from the coroner's office interrupted, “We've got a gun shot wound.” He had been squatting behind the victim's butt, with a small flashlight held between his teeth, while keeping his hands free to examine the only visible sign of trauma. Jeremy had placed the flashlight back into the black box and was starting to stand up when he made his proclamation. With a sense of self-satisfaction, he changed his rubber gloves.

Everyone else in the room stopped their work and listened to hear what the technician had to say next. Instead of volunteering his knowledge, Jeremy just stood there, adjusting each individual finger in his gloves. Each popped into place with an authoritative snap. Finally, Del Panetti couldn't wait any longer. He said, “Okay, boy. Spit it out. You've got our undivided attention.”

Jeremy reached into his black box and pulled out some extra gloves. He tossed a pair to Jackson, then Panetti, and finally handed a pair to Dunbar. “If you'll please put these gloves on and assist me in rolling the body over, I'll try to explain.”

The body was still a bit stiff, but rigor was passing. They rolled the body off the hassock and onto the floor. With a little effort, they were able to straighten out the victim's limbs. The front of the victim was as equally devoid of marks and wounds as the back, with two notable exceptions.

The first was the marked lividity of the skin due to blood pooling in the lower portions of the body upon death. The second was a tattoo on the victim's upper thigh.

Jeremy puzzled a bit then said, “Well, this isn't exactly what I had expected, but it doesn't change my opinion.”

Dunbar asked, “So professor. What is your opinion?”

"There is a gunshot wound on this victim. What's strange is that it is only an entry wound. There's no exit wound. At least I don't think so."

Panetti asked, "You telling us the bloody anus is the gunshot wound?"

"Yes. That's exactly what I'm telling you."

There was a collective grimace among the men, as the reality of what they were talking about sunk into their brains. Dunbar asked, "So what's your theory about this?"

One of the other crime scene technicians spoke, "I think this might help you develop a theory, Inspector." He handed Dunbar a short stack of magazines inside plastic bags marked 'evidence.' The magazines were homosexual in nature.

Dunbar rolled his eyes and huffed out, "Yeah. Right. I should have known. Okay, professor. We got us a gay boy here who picks up some other faggot in a bar or pisses off his boyfriend. They're up here doing the dirty deed when instead of the hot salami, he slips him some hot lead. That how I'm reading it."

There was another collective grimace and then Jackson leans over and whispers into Panetti's ear, "You've got to hand it to whoever did this. Sticking the muzzle up there makes for one hell of a silencer."

Chapter 15

"Okay folks. What have you got for me?" Inspector Dunbar always liked to walk in a few minutes late to the meetings he held. It wasn't a demonstration of power or anything. It simply eliminated the need for chitchat and let him get right to the material which interested him.

This particular meeting was the routine follow-up meeting he would hold a couple days after a murder. It gave all of the groups involved in the investigation a chance to share what information they had been able to gather. It also gave Dunbar, as lead investigator, the information he needed to determine what resources would be assigned to the case.

Josh continued, "Okay, this meeting is for the fag killed on Polk Street two nights ago. What have we gotten so far? Del, you kick it off."

"The victim was a 45 year old, white male named Bradley Lewis. He was born in Rutherford, New Jersey. Upon the father's death in 1934, he and his mother apparently moved to Hollywood and then Las Vegas, where she made a pretty good name for herself as a stripper. She died a few years ago in a nursing home. He had no brothers or sisters.

"Lewis served in Europe with the Army during World War II. Nothing unusual about his service record. The victim was a part-time actor, sometimes director in a few of the local theater productions. According to friends and neighbors, he was a known homosexual, but fairly discreet about it. Neighbors in the building had no complaints about him and heard nothing unusual during the day or night of the murder. No one saw anyone come or go. No wants. No warrants. Except for the obvious, he lived a pretty normal life."

Delano's last sentence caused a few snickers in the group, which Dunbar quickly cut off with, "Forensics. What have you got?"

Jeremy Williams put on his reading glasses and opened his three-ring binder which was stuffed with various forms, reports, and scraps of paper. Finding the page he needed, Jeremy started, "The victim was a white male, five foot eight inches tall and around 150 pounds.

Death was the result of massive internal injuries and bleeding from a gunshot through the anus."

Another set of snickers broke out and Dunbar asked, "What kind of gun was it?"

Someone in the back chirped, "A damned friendly one if you ask me."

Jeremy ignored the laughter and answered, "I have no idea, but I would say it was of some pretty decent caliber."

Delano puzzled, "What do you mean you're not sure. You said at the scene there wasn't an exit wound. Where's the slug?"

"That's just it," the technician continued. "There is no exit wound and there is no bullet. There isn't even a wound channel."

Dunbar cleared an area on his desk and pulled out his note pad before asking, "I'm sure you've developed some working theory here. What is it?"

"There's no doubt in my mind that the barrel of the gun was fully inserted into the victim's rectum."

"I bet it was," chuckled a member of the group. As much as he wanted to laugh himself, Josh quieted the group with an icy stare and then nodded for the technician to continue his report.

"There were no muzzle burns on the skin surrounding the anus. I'm thinking the weapon was a revolver, because there's no trauma to suggest the cycling of an automatic weapon's slide. The only external tissue damage was a symmetrical pattern of powder residue which would be consistent with gases escaping from a revolver's forcing cone."

The terms and words caused more giggles from the group. The technician paused, then continued, "The internal tissue damage was caused from the muzzle flash and burning gases from the gunpowder. Since there was no bullet, I'm thinking the gun must have been loaded with blanks.

"The gases destroyed the rectum, bladder, most of the small intestine, part of both kidneys, and destroyed both the descending aorta and the inferior vena cava. Officially, the victim bled to death and died of shock in a matter of seconds."

The kibitzer added, "I'll bet it was a shock."

Dunbar had had about enough. "Okay. All of you. If you've got any more jokes, get them out of your system now. I don't care how funny this is. In my office, we get serious. A gay, I mean guy, died and it's our job to walk this thing through. Got it? Now go ahead, Williams."

"From the amount of damage and estimating the amount of gas..." There were some held back laughs on that line. "...I'd say the weapon was at least a thirty-eight, maybe a forty-four special, or even a forty-five."

Dunbar switched over with, "Crime Scene. What do you have for me?"

One of the workers wiped laughing tears from his eyes and then said, "We basically got zilch. There were no fingerprints we haven't been able to account for. The killer either wore gloves or wiped everything down. No unusual footprints, fibers, or hairs. Like I said, we got zilch."

Dunbar wasn't happy with the answer, but resigned himself to the facts. Holding his arms and hands skyward, he asked, "Does anyone have anything to help me here?"

Everyone thought for moment and then Jeremy Williams said, "There is one other unusual thing, Inspector."

"And what might that be?"

"The guy had a tattoo."

Panetti said, "Yeah. I remember it. It was a bunch of words in a box. Sort of looked like a billboard."

Jeremy corrected, “When I examined the victim, it specifically read 'banque nationale du paris' with a small box around it.”

Inspector Dunbar seemed uninterested when he asked, “You find anything special about it?”

“Not specifically, but in French, it reads 'National Bank of Paris'. I thought you might want to call and see if this bank is in Paris and then...”

Dunbar rocked forward in his chair, shook his head, and said, “No, No, No. I'm not calling anyone. What am I going to say? Excuse me Mr. Banker, but I've got a dead body here with your label on it? I don't think so.”

Jeremy was unsure of his position in this group, so he replied, “I know it sounds weird, but didn't it strike you as unusual?”

“Who the hell knows. The guy was in World War II, maybe he got it then. Maybe it was a joke. For all I know it could be some homosexual thing.” Looking over the entire group, he continued, “Has anyone got anything important to add to our discussion?”

No hands were raised and no comments offered, only a collection of shaking heads and silly looks found their way to Dunbar. He signaled the end of the meeting and motioned everyone to leave the room. Inspector Panetti stayed behind and closed the door after the others. “What do you think, Josh?”

Dunbar huffed a sigh and leaned back in his chair, interlocking his fingers behind his head. He put his feet up on his desk and then said, “I think somebody's playtime got out of hand or this faggot's boyfriend got jealous. We've got no witnesses, no weapon, no fingerprints, and no case. I say we throw it in the pile and wait for some real evidence to show up.”

Chapter 16

"Why in the hell are we down here, Del?"

Inspector Panetti, obviously used to the moodiness of his partner and superior, tightened his collar against the cold wind blowing across the docks from off San Francisco Bay. Delano said, "Ain't my idea, Josh."

"So who was the moron who called me away from a perfectly good, and mind you, warm lunch to go dodging seagull droppings down here on the docks?"

"I got a call from the coroner's office saying there was something down here you might find interesting."

"Well, hey, why didn't you tell me it was a murder?"

Del paused for a minute and then said, "I didn't say it was a murder. Actually, Jerry said it was an industrial accident."

Inspector Dunbar stopped in his tracks and asked, "You mean the snot-nosed, know-it-all kid from Chicago who a few weeks back wanted me to call Paris because of that guy's tattoo?"

"Yeah."

Resuming his walk with a bit more energy, Inspector Dunbar fumed. "This better be good, or I'll kick his little ass. You know he's been nothing but a pain in the butt, no pun intended, since we worked the murder on Polk Street."

"Yeah, I know Josh, but he called me and said some guy died in an accident on the docks. He said there was something you'd want to see. He probably figured calling me was smarter than trying to talk you into coming down here himself."

"Well, he got that one right. I'd have told him to take a hike."

The two inspectors continued their walk along the pier until they reached the small crowd of workers, reporters, and official people surrounding a crane on the dock. Pushing their way through the mob, they eventually broke through and ran into the coroner and his crew.

Jeremy Williams pulled off the rubber glove on his right hand and reached out, saying, “Inspector Dunbar. I'm glad you could make it down here.”

Josh had his hands in his pockets for warmth, and he left them there, leaving the poor coroner's hand naked to the elements. About the time Jeremy's hand lowered, Dunbar said, “So, why am I down here for an industrial accident?”

A bit insulted, the Coroner said, “I'm not so sure this is an accident.”

“What do you mean? It's either an accident or it isn't.”

“It looks like an accident. Actually, I won't be able to tell you for sure until I get the body back into the lab and do the work-up.”

Becoming agitated, Inspector Dunbar started moving and looking around as he said, “You don't know if this is an accident or not, but you dragged my butt down here. I don't even see the body. Where the hell is it?”

The Coroner replaced the rubber glove on his hand and with a slightly smirky grin he pointed toward the edge of the dock and said, “The body's over there.”

“I don't see anything? Stop playing games with me. Where's the body?”

Chuckling a little bit, Jeremy said, “No. It's there. Under the blue sheet.”

About fifty feet away, was a blue vinyl tarp spread flat on the ground. There didn't appear to be anything under it. Dunbar's curiosity was now hooked. Walking toward it with the coroner, Josh asked, "You're telling me there's a body under there?"

"That I am."

"Squashed flat?"

"Like a pancake," nodded the coroner.

"This I got to see."

The pair arrived at the body and pulled back the tarp. The smell was almost overwhelming. "Phew!" said Dunbar putting his handkerchief over his mouth and nose. "How long has this been sitting here?"

Jeremy held out an opened jar of Vicks Vap-o-rub to Inspector Dunbar. Josh thanked the coroner as he took a finger full and shoved it up his nose to cover the stench. Jeremy closed the jar and put it in his pocket before saying, "Best guess I've heard is three or four days. Could be more."

Fascinated by the flattened corpse, Dunbar asked, "How did this happen?"

Pointing to the ground around the body, the coroner answered, "If you look at the dock, you'll see a large rectangle of cracked and chipped concrete. Seems someone dropped a cargo container on him."

Dunbar felt the cracked concrete and cringed a bit. "Geesh. You mean those big shipping crates? The ones they lift off ships and then put onto rail cars or semi-trucks?"

"Yup. One of those big ones. A pretty heavy one too."

Dunbar stood up and yelled over to his partner, "Del! Start asking questions. I want to know who this poor schmuck was and who knows anything about what happened." Delano Panetti nodded and went about his business.

The coroner tapped Dunbar on the shoulder and said, "I know who the victim was."

Still fascinated with the body, he told the coroner, "Look at this. The damned container must have smashed his arm into mush. One of his arms is missing."

"No," said the coroner, "He was already missing the arm."

"What?"

"Yeah. The guy's name was Cummings, Randy Cummings, but they tell me his nickname was Sarge. They told me his lost his arm back in 1960. Got it caught between a truck and a crate. They said something about a crane accident on the loading dock. Crushed it off right at the shoulder, they say."

"Well he wasn't so lucky this time."

Having somewhat satisfied his grisly curiosity for the time being, Dunbar returned to the circumstances of the incident and why he was called. "So, this poor guy is walking along and the cable snaps on one of these containers. It falls on him and we need a pancake flipper to scrape him up. Sounds like an accident to me. Why'd you call Homicide?"

Thinking Dunbar should have figured it out himself, the Coroner was a bit frustrated as he explained. "No one reported the accident. No one found the body until they came to move the container this morning."

"Yeah, so what?"

"Can you imagine the noise this thing must have made when it hit the ground? If there were people around, don't you think someone would have noticed?"

Dunbar yielded a bit, saying, "Okay, I see your point. My question though, is how'd this guy get under the container? If no one else was around, like you say, I doubt this guy would have been standing around waiting for the crane operator to drop a container on him. Still sounds a lot like an accident to me."

"When I get the body back to the lab, I'll know more. Maybe he was knocked unconscious and laid here until the killer could hook up the crane. The way the body is squashed, I'd say this Sarge guy wasn't standing, but was probably lying face down on the ground."

Looking back down at the body, Dunbar thought about it for a moment and then said, "I see what you mean, but so far, all you've got are suspicions. You keep telling me you won't have firm answers until you get back to the shop. You still haven't told me why I got called in."

Straightening himself up and looming in front of the coroner, Dunbar pointed his finger at Jeremy's chest and continued, "Standard procedures say you don't call us until you are reasonably certain there has been foul play in the death. So, why'd you call Homicide and why did I have the distinct honor of being called personally, by you?"

The coroner took his hand and gently lowered the Inspector's finger. His hand then continued its movement, reaching into his coat pocket and pulling out a rubber glove, which he held out to Dunbar. The Inspector had a puzzled look on his face as he accepted the glove. A grin of retribution spread across Jeremy's face as he told the Inspector, "Pull down the dead man's pants."

"You've got to be kidding me."

"You think I called you down here for nothing. Why should I explain what you can see for yourself? Pull down the man's pants."

Dunbar put on the rubber glove and bent over the flattened body. He reluctantly pulled at the blue jeans, drenched with body fluids and sticking to the decaying flesh. Eventually he got the pants down far enough to expose the buttocks. What he saw made him whistle, "Well, I'll be damned."

"Not a bad thought," replied a sarcastic coroner. "I came across it during my preliminary examination of the body. I'm sorry Inspector, but as soon as I saw it, I thought of you. Seemed too much of a coincidence if you ask me."

Dunbar blinked his eyes in disbelief, but the image remained. A bit discolored from the trauma, but none the less clearly visible on the flattened cheek was a tattoo. It read "banque nationale du paris".

Chapter 17

Inspector Dunbar opened the door into the conference room. The noise and activity within the room immediately came to a stop. With his coffee cup in hand, he headed toward the desk at the head of the room, saying, "Okay boys and girls, what do we have on the table today?"

No one really came to the fore, so he found someone to start. "Fine. I'll start. What have we got on the human pancake found on the docks? Del, what have we got as far as background and witnesses?"

"Victim's name was Randolph Cummings. He was forty-eight years old, divorced, no kids, and was working as a crew foreman for one of the warehouse companies. He's been working the docks for almost twenty years. Nothing unusual about his work record. His father worked for the same company before retiring a few years ago."

"Are his parents still alive?" asked Dunbar.

"Both are still living here in San Francisco. They were out in Nebraska as part of a vacation they were taking, driving around the Midwest. Once they were notified, they started back to San Francisco. They're expected to be back some time today."

"Good. Del, you and I will go out to interview them, once they get here and as soon as they're ready for it."

"Okay, Josh."

"Anything else about his work record?"

Del continued through his notes, "No, that's about it for work. You already knew about the loss of his arm. Totally an accident. There was some talk of him going on disability, but the company and their insurance company felt it was better to make him a foreman than to pay the claims."

"Was anyone at the company out to get this guy?"

"None that I found. Everyone seemed to love him. They called him Sarge and really seemed to go out of their way to tell me what a nice guy he was."

Dunbar asked, "Where'd this guy's nickname come from? Was he in the war?"

"Served in World War II as a sergeant. Earned a couple of Bronze Stars for heroism. They wanted him to go to non-commissioned officer school, but he was happy staying a line sergeant and turned them down. He got an honorable discharge at the end of the war. Nothing unusual."

"Did anyone on the docks see or hear anything?" Josh asked.

"No one saw anything! Not one thing. A couple of people were concerned as to why he hadn't reported to work as scheduled on the day his body was found, but he'd been scheduled off work for four days prior to it."

"So what you're telling me is we have no real idea when this accident happened? When was the cargo container unloaded?"

"We did check on it, boss," answered Delano. "The container came in with a shipment of machine tools two weeks ago on some Korean freighter. It was off-loaded the same day and was sitting around until the other day when it was being picked up to be loaded onto a train for shipment to the East coast. Could have happened any time in between."

"Great," huffed Dunbar. Looking over to Jeremy, the coroner, Josh said, "Well, looks like the game is in your ballpark to tell us when this all happened. What have you got for me, rookie?"

Ignoring the jab at his relatively new status to the San Francisco police department, the coroner said, "As you can imagine, the condition of the body has made an exact determination a little bit difficult. We're still waiting on some test results, but I'm pretty sure he'd been under the container for less than seventy-two hours, but more than twenty-four."

"Now we're getting somewhere. That puts the death some time between Tuesday and Thursday. Del, do we have a list of employees scheduled to work those days?"

"Yeah, boss, but they won't do you much good."

"And why is that?"

Del continued his thought, "That particular company only has a small number of regular employees. Some evenings, if things are slow, there's only one or two of them working."

Dunbar was a bit confused. "You mean it only takes one or two of them to unload a ship?"

"No. I'm not saying that at all. They hire a lot of day-laborers, off the books. They'll pick up whoever and however many they need to get the workload done for the day. They've been paying them in cash, so they don't even have their names."

"Damn! Okay, rookie. That's strike one. What else have you got on this Sarge guy?"

Jeremy returned to his notes and stated, "Mr. Cummings was about six feet tall and weighed about two hundred pounds. I'm afraid I can't be any more exact than that given the circumstances. I was correct in my original assumption that the victim was lying on the ground, face down, before the container was dropped on him."

Dunbar broke in with, "Could you tell if he was dead before the container was dropped on him?"

"They tell me the container weighed thirty-six thousand pounds and my guess is it was dropped from at least fifty feet in the air. There is normally a small gap under the container of about six-inches, to accommodate getting lifting straps and such under them, but this thing hit with such force, the feet imbedded in the concrete.

"This man's skull was crushed, as were most of the major structures in his body. I'd say there was no part of his body left, that was more than an inch thick. This made most normal ways of determining such things impossible."

"Thanks for the physics lesson, but I asked you if he was dead before the thing was dropped on him."

"I did some microscopic analysis of the tissues and I'm pretty sure he was alive when the box fell. He wasn't bound or tied, and I think we can agree no one would voluntarily wait under a large container for it to drop, so I am assuming the victim was unconscious at the time."

Inspector Dunbar asked, "Are you saying he was drugged, or are you telling me he was knocked out?"

"There were no unusual drugs in his system, but there was enough time for some of them to clear his system. There wasn't enough intact brain material to determine if there was a concussion caused by a blow to knock him unconscious."

"What are you telling me?"

"I'm telling you there's no hard evidence available to prove he was murdered. As much as I hate to say so, this still could have been an accident. I can't rule it out."

"Strike two!" screamed Dunbar. "You people never cease to amaze me. Anybody else who wants to step up to the plate?"

No one else in the room wanted to get involved unless they absolutely had to. After a few minutes, the coroner raised his hand and asked, “What about the tattoo?”

“I thought we went through this with the last guy. What about the tattoo?”

Jeremy energetically challenged, “Doesn't it strike you as the least bit strange we've got two dead bodies with identical tattoos?”

“Yes it does. It's damned strange, but if you haven't figured this out yet, you're working in San Francisco and there are always a lot of weird things going on here. All you've told me is I have one murder and one accident, and there isn't a shred of evidence at this point which ties the two together. What's the link?”

Jeremy thought for a minute and said, “I don't know right now, but I think we should at least continue to look into this.”

“We will continue to look into this. It is by no means closed, but if you are suggesting to me that I call Paris because of those damned tattoos, my answer is the same as last time. No!”

Chapter 18

The Los Angeles police department lieutenant heading up the stakeout keyed his microphone and asked, “So, how's it going, Legs?”

Detective Laura Miles tossed her full, heavily teased, blond hair and whispered into her hidden microphone, “It looks like our target is heading my way. Everyone get ready for my signal.”

Detective Miles made the perfect decoy. The jokes around the precinct house referred to her as “Detective

Laura with the Miles of thighs." She was five foot ten inches tall, with a body which simply would not quit.

Laura was leaning against a bus stop shelter. Silhouetted against the harsh street lights, she was hard to miss. There was nothing between her six inch high heels and the hem of her hot pink, stretch miniskirt except her most striking feature, long, slender, dancer's legs. The elastic cinched in her already tiny waist and marked the next division of bare skin, up to where the equally hot pink, bikini top held in her ample cleavage.

Having no other place to really hide a radio and microphone, Detective Miles wore an unzipped, short leather jacket. A few large gold bracelets and big dangling ear rings finished her disguise. The drug dealing pimp they were trying to catch saw nothing but another "working girl" he could add to his collection. Over the open transmitter, her fellow officers could hear the conversation as they prepared to spring the trap.

"Yo. Babe. What's up?"

Chewing her gum, she dispassionately asked, "What's it to you?"

"Oh baby. Don't be so cold. Maybe I can help you."

"Yeah, well I've heard that before."

The pimp slid up next to her and looked over her merchandise. Liking what he saw, he said, "You are incredibly fine, but you know I'm not here to make time with you. Word has it, some really leggy bitch was looking for me to deal some coke."

Detective Laura ran her hands through her hair before looking him in the eye and asking, "Are you Sweet?"

Stepping back and bowing slightly to her, he said, "At your service. If you are looking for meat or treat, the man you seek is Sweet."

Laura smiled and chuckled slightly. "You're a poet and don't even know it. Is that it?"

Sweet showed his two gold front teeth when he smiled back at her. "Now that's better, baby. You and I should be friends. With your legs and my management, we could both make a lot of bread."

"So you're telling me you're connected?" she asked.

"Baby, whatever you want, I can get it."

Laura stood up and asked, "Weren't you supposed to bring a sample with you?"

Sweet took off his hat and pulled out a fairly sizable amount of white powder in a plastic bag. He held it out to the detective and said, "Take a taste of this. It is some really fine shit."

Laura Miles took the bag and opened it. Using the long nail on her pinkie finger, she dipped into the bag and pulled out small pile of the powder. Tasting it, she agreed to the quality of the product. "How much can I get and when?"

"What I've got ain't the problem. Unless you've got the world's biggest pussy to hide it, you ain't got the cash. I've got two keys waiting in my car. If you've got the cash, I've got the shit."

Detective Miles stood in front of Sweet and spread the stance of her legs slightly. Sweet whistled at the view he had of her legs. Laura reached her arms out and pulled him to her. Sweet loved the attention. As she leaned into him, she slid her arms around, up his back, and whispered the signal to the cops and into Sweet's ears. "Isn't there something else you'd like before I get you the cash?"

The police cars began to roll, closing in on the corner. Sweet started to squeeze the detective and kiss her, when he sensed the net closing on him. Before he could get loose, Laura kneed him in the groin, spun him around sideways bringing her knee up into his chin. As Sweet staggered, Detective Miles shifted her weight and spinning, back-kicked him in the chest. As he fell unconscious to the ground, she said, "You're under arrest."

She had just finished handcuffing Sweet when her lieutenant came up to her, holstering his gun. "You scare the shit out of me every time you do it."

Pulling her skirt down and readjusting her clothes, she said, "Yeah, I know, but where's the guy going to go when I've got my arms around him?"

"Some day, one of these guys is going to go right through you. That's what worries me. One day your luck is going to run out."

Putting her hand on his neck in a friendly gesture, she laughed and said, "Hey, I appreciate it, but after tonight, you don't have to worry about it any more."

The lieutenant patted her on the back and said, "We're going to miss you on Vice, but I know how much you've been wanting to work Homicide. You are the sexiest decoy I've ever had."

"Thanks, Lieutenant. I might even miss doing this gig. I do have to admit tonight was a lot of fun. I can't think of any better way to go out, than to nail a scum bag like Sweet."

As they headed back to her car, she passed the prisoner. Sweet was still bent over slightly, in pain, but Laura leaned over and kissed him on the cheek, saying, "No hard feelings."

The lieutenant said, "Well, you take the rest of the weekend off. We'll expect you in Homicide, first thing Monday morning."

Laura unlocked the door of her car and replied, "Thanks for everything you've taught me. I do have just one last question, though."

"What's that?"

"When I report to Homicide, will I still get to wear these stylish clothes?"

Chapter 19

Homicide Detective Laura Miles pulled up in front of Carter's Pawn Shop. A dozen marked squad cars were already there and the area was cordoned off from the general public. The revolving magnetic red light atop her car's roof, let the patrolman guarding the entrance know to let her unmarked vehicle through the barricades.

She had looked forward to this day, the day she would head up a homicide investigation. It was one thing to work with others, you always did that. It was another thing to work as an assistant to the training officer who was showing you the ropes. It was quite another thing to lead your own investigation and make all of the critical decisions alone. It can get pretty cold out on the limb when you're in charge.

Even though she was no longer wearing the short skirts and revealing costumes she did while working vice, she could hardly help causing a momentary pause in the men's actions, whenever she got out of the car. It was rare for a woman to reach her level in the police department. She earned every bit of the respect and every promotion along the way.

There were still those who thought she "slept her way to the top." There was nothing she could do about their opinions, but do the best job she could and hope their opinions would change over time. Still, the novelty of a female detective and a beautiful one at that, always caused a stir at the scene of a crime.

Laura threw the gear selector of her car into park, unbuckled her seat belt and got out of the car. She was wearing dark slacks and a muted blouse. Both were covered by her trench coat, unbuttoned and open, as the day was beginning to warm up. As she strode past the patrolmen outside the pawn shop, she still looked more like a runway model than a serious cop. She knew it. She also knew it made it necessary for her to take charge inside, as soon as possible.

The door to the pawn shop was open, so she walked into the middle of the shop and in her most authoritative voice said, "Detective Miles here. Homicide. Who was first on the scene?"

An officer turned from his duties and walked up to her. Respecting her superior title he said, "I'm Officer Williams. My partner, Sergeant Green, and I got the call about nine o'clock this morning. It wasn't until we got the safe open that we knew it was a homicide. We called in your department about noon."

"What do you mean you didn't know it was a homicide until someone opened the safe?"

"The body was in the safe, detective."

Realizing everyone probably thought she should have made the obvious connection herself, Laura backed up a bit to regain control of the situation. "I realized it was probably the case, officer. I was asking why YOU didn't make the connection for three hours."

Feeling the edge to her voice, the officer said, "Sorry detective."

"Fine," said Detective Miles. "Let's start at the beginning. Tell me what you did."

The officer said, "We got the call about nine. Dispatch called it a burglary. We were ten blocks away. It took us five minutes to arrive, where we found the citizen who called it in."

"Was it the shop owner?"

"No, actually the shop owner turned out to be the victim."

"So who was the caller?"

"One Melvin Shumaker. He's the accountant for the business. He found the business locked about eight o'clock this morning, which he claims was unusual."

"Why was it unusual? I saw the hours sign when I walked in. It says this shop is open from ten to midnight."

The officer flipped open his notebook and continued, "The accountant said he meets with the owner every Wednesday morning to go over the books. He says the guy never misses and leaves the door unlocked. Mr. Shumaker also said there was a handwritten note in the window saying the owner was on vacation until next week."

"Okay, so that explains why the door was locked."

"Not according to the accountant. He knew for a fact the owner was not on vacation and on this particular Wednesday morning, they were going to be going over the shop's income tax returns. This was supposed to be a major meeting. He seriously doubted the owner would forget about it."

Detective Miles looked around the shop. It looked like every other pawn shop in the area. Musical instruments and appliances covered every inch of shelf space and were hanging from the ceiling everywhere. Glass cases filled with guns, gold, and jewelry lined the back wall. She asked, "So, what did the accountant do then?"

"Figuring there was some mix up, he decided to let himself in with his own key and wait for the owner. He figured it was better to wait inside than to stand around this neighborhood in an expensive suit."

"Sounds smart to me," she said.

"So the accountant comes in and the first thing to hit him was the smell."

Detective Miles caught the scent of the dead body outside the shop. Decaying human bodies have a distinctive smell. You never forget it or get used to it, but homicide personnel learn to tolerate it or they get out. Fortunately for Laura, a little extra bit of her perfume was enough to make it bearable. She asked, "And then what?"

"The accountant at first figured something died in a mousetrap or out back in the alley. See the smell was seeping out around the door of the safe, so it wasn't as strong then."

Taking another look around, she asked, "Your original call was for a burglary. Nothing seems out of the ordinary. What tipped off the accountant?"

The officer turned the page of his notebook and said, "The bean counter said he was just starting to lay out his books on the counter when he noticed the jewelry was out of order."

"What do you mean out of order?"

"That's what I asked. It seems he and the owner had a specific way to lay out their merchandise to make taking inventory easier. They kept rings in one area, watches in another, then necklaces and such. That way they could just work right to left or something like that."

"So, someone had been through the jewelry. Was anything missing?"

"He couldn't tell at first, so he whipped out the records from the previous week, compared them and nothing seemed too far off. Then to be sure, he checks the cash register."

"Let me guess. The cash was still in the drawer."

A bit puzzled, the officer says, "Yeah. The money was still in the drawer. How did you know?"

Acting a little bit smug, Detective Miles said, "So far, nothing about this is making sense, so I figured a burglary call with nothing missing was a natural. Can you get to the point?"

Returning to his notes, the officer said, "Well, the money was in the cash register, but there were no bills bigger than the fives. That is what made him suspicious. So, he looked into a shoe box the owner kept stashed under the cash register and it was empty."

"Why is that significant?"

"The accountant said it was the owner's secret stash. You know, when someone brings in something big to pawn, maybe for a few hundred dollars. According to the accountant, there would normally be five hundred bucks in the box."

"Why would the owner keep five hundred dollars in a box when there's a perfectly good safe right behind him?"

Raising his finger into the air as if he had one over on the detective, the officer said, "I asked him the same question. Seems the owner kept the safe open during business hours and in plain view. He figured a big locked safe was too tempting to robbers. The safe was only for business records."

Understanding things a bit better now, she said, "Let me see if I've got it. The accountant figured someone carefully went thought the merchandise and then put it back in the case, but left with the cash?"

"Yeah. Then he calls us because he figured it was a burglary and that's when we got here. We smelled the dead body, but couldn't find it. Finally we figured out it was coming from inside the safe."

"Didn't the accountant have the combination?"

"You'd have thought so," replied the officer. "We had to call in a locksmith. It took him a good hour to get here and then another hour to open the door. When that door swung open, you should have smelled it."

"No thanks. What's left is enough for me. Looks like you've done a thorough job. Can I see the body now?"

As they began walking over to the counter in front of the safe, Officer Green, the partner of the reporting patrolman came up to them and said, "Hey Bob. Do you know who the shop owner is?"

Being polite, Officer Williams intervened with, "John, this is Detective Miles. Detective Miles, this is my partner, Sergeant Green. This case has been assigned to Detective Miles."

The detective and the sergeant knew each other, but the junior officer could not have known. The sergeant held out his hand to shake hers, saying, "Nice to see you again, Laura. So, you finally got your wish and you're in Homicide now. Congratulations."

Shaking his hand, she answered him with, "Thanks, John. Still breaking in the rookies I see."

Sergeant Green winked at Officer Williams and then replied to Laura with, "Somebody's got to do it. Might as well make sure it gets done right."

Williams asked, "So what were you saying about the victim?"

"Yeah, this shopkeeper has an interesting history. His name is George Carter. Nice guy. Little guy. About five foot four. Absolutely bald head. Not a hair on it."

Laura asked, "How'd you know him?"

"I used to walk this beat about ten years ago. The neighborhood was a lot different then. George's father was a cop, until he got shot in the leg. Then his dad took a disability pension. His mother worked in an aircraft factory during the war."

"Nice story," said the detective, "but what's so interesting about it?"

"George never was much of an achiever. His dad was embarrassed by his lack of drive. George made a living scrounging."

"What the hell is scrounging?" asked Officer Williams.

"You know. He'd buy junk things cheap, fix them up and sell them for a profit. He had this nickname of Moocher. Neighbors would come to him if they were looking for something cheap."

Detective Miles was getting impatient with the reminiscing and said, "Okay, so the guy was a lazy bum and his dad didn't like it. What's so interesting about it?"

"When George's father was shot and had to leave the force, George tried to become a cop. He didn't meet the minimum height requirement, but it didn't stop him from trying. Every time we had an academy class open, he applied. Finally he gave up and opened this shop with his dad."

"Okay, so now we know how he got this pawn shop. What difference does it make?"

"About eight years ago, some hood came into the shop to hold it up. The robbery went bad and George's dad got killed. George vowed to find the perp before the cops and kill the guy himself."

"That's understandable," said Williams.

"Yeah, well a few days later the robber is found dead in the alley out behind the shop with about twenty, forty-five caliber bullet holes through him. We figured it had to be a Thompson sub-machine gun. George happened to have one in his shop and it was freshly cleaned. Ballistics matched the bullets that killed the perp to the Thompson."

Laura said, "Sounds like an open and shut case of revenge. Why wasn't this guy rotting in prison?"

Sergeant Green said, "There were no witnesses. It was a hot summer night and more than a dozen apartments have windows and balconies facing the alley. No one claimed to see anything. George claimed to have bought the gun off someone the same night for a hundred dollars. The district attorney's office figured prosecuting such a sympathetic character, without witnesses, for the sake of some hoodlum wasn't worth it. Besides that, it was revenge on a cop-killer, so they let it drop."

"So, are you telling me this because you think someone else was getting revenge on this Carter character years later?"

"Hey. It was a thought. Want to see the body now?'"

Laura motioned to the counter and walked with the officers to the back wall. In a break between the counters, she could see the coroner and a technician kneeling down in front of the safe. When she got there, they both stood up and unblocked her view.

George Carter was stuffed into the safe, naked. His nakedness was made more prominent due to his bald head. Moocher was really, really naked, from head to toe. He had been sitting in the safe, his knees pulled up in front of him, his arms around his knees. When the door was opened, one of his hands fell to the floor, its fist clenched as if it were reaching for an invisible gear shift knob.

Laura couldn't resist the moment and joked, "He looks like one of my high-school bus drivers."

The men laughed at her joke and then returned to their work. Sgt. Green introduced Laura to the coroner and then she asked, "So Doc, what do you think happened here?"

The coroner matter of factly said, "Suffocation. Plain and simple. We figure the burglar must have surprised him or something, made him strip naked, and then shut him in the safe. Nasty way to go. If the safe were airtight, he would have died in minutes. There was enough air seeping around the door that it might have taken hours. Poor devil."

Detective Miles asked, "What's this mark on his butt?"

The coroner said, "It's a tattoo. Nothing special about it. Why?"

"I used to work vice and I got to know most of the tattoo parlor operators in the area. Can you get me an extra photo of the tattoo? I may be able to show it around and see where it came from."

The coroner nodded and said, "Hey, whatever turns you on."

Chapter 20

Inspector Dunbar was soaking in some of San Diego's famous sunshine. The warm sun of southern California was such a contrast to the typically cold and cloudy days of his San Francisco. He turned to one of his fellow police officers and said, "God, I just love it when they hold these conventions down here. I swear it's the only time in my life I don't feel cold."

San Diego was hosting the annual California convention for homicide investigators. It was a chance for officers to get together and discuss their common issues, see the latest in crime-fighting equipment, but more importantly for Josh, it was a chance to get away and blow off some steam. The Hotel del Coronado was the perfect setting in one of the most perfect spots on earth.

Josh was just about ready to call it a day and go back inside, when he heard a small commotion and the whistles of at least a dozen policemen. He sat up to see what was going on, only to see the most perfect vision walking his way. He also couldn't help letting out a sigh.

He thought to himself, "What a body!" The woman walking toward him was striking to say the least. Tall and blond like most of California girls, she was wearing dark sunglasses, a thin white robe wafting open in the breeze, and a tiny red bikini. You could see the men's heads turn as she walked by and you could hear the sucking sound of middle-aged cops pulling their bellies in tight.

As the woman drew nearer, her head turned toward him and she slowed down. Finally, she stopped in front of him, pulled her sunglasses down a bit and peered over them at Inspector Dunbar. She asked, "Josh? Is it really you?"

When he saw her eyes, he recognized the woman and stood up. "Well, I'll be damned. Laura Miles. How the hell have you been?"

They paused for a moment and then embraced each other. There was a collective rush of wind caused by a hundred exhales and a communal sigh of disappointment from the crowd. They parted and each sat on the edge of a different beach chair, facing each other. Dunbar spoke first, saying, "Wow. It seems like ages since I've seen you. How have you been and why are you here?"

Laura chuckled and replied, "I've been fine and you're going to get a good laugh out of why I'm here."

"Why? Are you working here at the hotel?"

"No. I'm a homicide detective."

Josh was shocked, to say the least, and sat for a moment with his mouth hanging open. He shook his head in disbelief and asked, "You? You became a police officer?"

Laura nodded in slight embarrassment and said, "Hard to believe, isn't it?"

"I'll say. You used to give me such grief back in college about my wanting to go into police work. Now you're a cop. What happened to the theater idea of yours?"

"Oh, I got my degree in theater, but when I tried to find work as a dancer or an actress, I ran into the darker side of show business you used to talk about. All I ever got was propositions from smelly old men who said they might be able to help me if I'd help them first. You'd think Los Angeles would be a great place to find work, but if you're a dancer you've either got to go to New York or Las Vegas. One was a place I didn't want to live and the other was a type of dancing I didn't like."

Josh laughed and said, "I told you it would be harder than you thought."

"Hey, don't rub it in. Besides, I got tired of the hours of practice and eating like a bird to keep my weight down, so I walked away from it."

Josh raised her arms slightly with his, looked at her and said, "You must still be eating like a bird. The years have been very good to you. You look fantastic."

She blushed slightly at the comment from an old friend and smiled, "You always knew the right words to make a girl happy."

Josh let her arms drop and then asked, "So why did you go into police work?"

"Actually, I sort of stumbled into it. I was on an interview for what was listed as a dancing job, but it turned out to be some creep doing pornography. I stormed out of there the minute I found out what was going on."

"Must have disappointed the guy."

"I'm sure it did, but it really ticked me off, so I went to the police and as luck had it, they'd been trying to put this particular creep away, so they asked me to help. The cops dressed me to a tee, coached me on what to say, and sent me back in with a tape recorder in my purse. I got what they wanted and the cops put the guy away."

"Were you scared at all?"

She thought about it for a second and then replied, "You know, I really wasn't. I guess I was so mad at this guy, I didn't think about it. Well anyway, the police were so impressed with the way I did it, they asked me if I'd be interested in doing this kind of thing for them. One thing led to another and then they sent me to the academy and I swung right into working vice and narcotics. For the first time, being a good looking woman paid off."

"Literally or figuratively?"

"Cut the crap, Dunbar! If anyone should know me, you should. You know I don't sleep around."

"You slept with me."

She pointed her finger and reminded him, "That was different. We were going to school and sharing an apartment with three other people. Besides, how many months did you try to bed me before I finally gave in?"

"Don't make it sound like a siege. That is, unless you want to admit you were some starry-eyed, gold-digging sophomore totally enthralled by a sexy senior."

Laura laughed at his remark and said, "Don't give yourself so much credit."

"That sounds like a regret to me."

Laura patted his hand and said, "No, Josh. We had some great times. I willingly gave you my virginity and those were the best six months in my life. We parted friends at the end of the year and I've never regretted it. You'll always have a warm spot in my heart."

Now Josh was a bit embarrassed. "Those were some great times. So, why are you here for this meeting if you're working vice?"

"I was working it, but a few months ago I got promoted and transferred over to Homicide. I fell in love with piecing together the puzzles and figuring out who the killer is. I've been looking forward to this meeting to help get me caught up on the learning curve."

"It's a damned small world, isn't it? After all these years we end up working in the same kind of job. Who would have thought?"

"Yeah. I'm working for the LAPD. How about you?"

"San Francisco. I moved up there to be closer to my family."

Laura looked at Josh's skin which was beginning to turn a bright shade of red. "You'd better get out of the sun. I guess those San Francisco days don't give you much of a tan."

Josh pushed a finger into his red skin and noticed the bright white spot left when he removed it. "Damn. You're right. I've got to go, but let's have dinner tonight. We can catch up on the rest of our lives then. How about it?"

"Sounds great to me. I wasn't looking forward to eating alone tonight and fighting off a hundred horny cops at the same time. I'm in room 124. You want to stop by about seven?"

"Seven it is. Got to go or they'll be serving me up as lobster for dinner tonight."

Chapter 21

Josh Dunbar raised his glass to Laura and said, "Here's to old times."

Laura raised hers, tapped the rims together and said, "Here's to old times and new beginnings." They both lowered their glasses and sipped their wine. Laura noticed Josh's face as she peered at him over the glass. "Did I say something wrong?"

Realizing he must have telegraphed his surprise, Josh composed himself and then replied, "No. I was just distracted there for a moment."

The waiter brought a basket of bread to the table and then took their dinner order. Josh offered the basket to Laura, who politely refused saying, "Don't get me started on that stuff. Bread goes straight to my thighs and if I eat just one slice, I'll finish the whole basket."

"I'd almost forgotten that about you. In school you practically lived on the stuff. Do you remember the night you tried using bread to forget being dumped by a boyfriend? A couple of us came home from the movies and found you curled up on the couch with a big loaf of French bread and a huge jar of jelly."

Laura laughed and then added, "Well, a loaf of bread never cheated on me with some honey bun."

Josh just shook his head and took another drink of wine. He swallowed the liquid and a bit of his pride to ask, "So, how many men have proposed to you along the way?"

"How does the old saying go?" thought Laura. "Oh yes, many men have tried, but none have succeeded."

"What? Are you telling me no one ever talked you into marriage?"

It was Laura's turn to take a sip of wine to cover her anxiety before she said, "What can I say? When I was in the theater, everyone tried to hit on me and a dozen older guys tried to wine and dine me into the sack. A few even talked grandly about whisking me away and getting married, but I never took them seriously. I didn't trust anybody then."

"So, what happened after that?" The waiter showed up with their salads and the conversation had to pause while plates were exchanged and questions about the dinner service were answered. Laura took a bite of her salad just as Josh asked, "Come on. What happened after that?"

She raised a finger to signal the need to empty her mouth before continuing. After she swallowed, Laura said, "Once I became a cop and started working vice and prostitution, I spent so much time with scum bags, I didn't have much time for men outside of work. I guess my lack of trust followed me into this work, too."

"I can't believe someone hasn't been able to break through and get inside. In all these years, I figured you to have had a couple of kids by now."

Laura almost choked on the bite she had in her mouth. "Me with kids? You have got to be kidding. Kids are just anchors holding you back. Right now I'm enjoying my freedom. Maybe down the road. Maybe someday, but not yet."

The waiter returned with their entrees, exchanged plates, and made more inquiries into the service. Josh looked at the meal and rolled his eyes at the almost smothering service and attention they were getting. He asked, "This is a far cry from the burgers and such we force down at work, isn't it."

"You can say that again." Laura took a bite of her meal and then asked Josh, "So what about you, old man. How many kids do you have?"

Now Josh choked a bit on his food. He wiped his lip and cleaned up the bits of food he had blown out of his mouth. He swallowed and then said, "You know I'm no more a fan of kids than you are."

"That's a shocker. You? You're such a skirt chaser. Your hormones were raging back in school. As horny as you were, I figured you to have married the first woman who would have you."

Josh replied, "I didn't marry you, did I?"

"Yeah, well I wasn't the first and I wouldn't have you. Back then, we were just play toys for each other."

"Maybe I should have taken you more seriously." Josh paused for a moment to judge Laura's reaction. There was no change in her expression, but his reply turned more somber. "You're right. I latched onto the first woman who wanted me and we got married almost immediately."

Laura became more serious, realizing it was a touchy subject for Josh. "Sounds like it didn't work out."

"I don't blame her. I was selfish. The working hours were hell. I don't think she was ready to handle being married to a policeman. Slowly, we started grating on each other. It got to the point where I started asking for stakeout duty so I wouldn't have to go home."

"So what finally happened?"

"I came home one night and she was gone, along with all of the furniture. No arguments. Just a letter over the fireplace. There were no fights at the divorce. She simply went her way and I went mine."

Laura paused for a second and said, "I'm sorry to hear it. I really am. You deserve better."

The waiter came to pick up their dishes, offered them coffee which they accepted, and then left the bill. Laura started to reach for the bill, but Josh stopped her. "I'll get this. It's the least I can do for making you listen to my sad story."

While they were waiting for the waiter to return with the change, Josh turned to Laura and forced out, "To tell you the truth, some of the happiest days of my life were with you. There was honesty between us. No games."

The long pause Josh's statement caused seemed to last forever, until it was broken by the returning money. Laura took a deep, long drink of her remaining wine as if she were avoiding something. She put the glass down and then said, "My. It seems a bit warm in here all of a sudden. Let's get some air."

The two stood up and walked out of the restaurant and into the open courtyard of the hotel. The air was a bit cool, now that the sun had gone down. Along the ocean, the sea breeze quickly returns to the temperature of the water, which is normally about sixty degrees. Laura's sheer blouse was not enough against the cold, so Josh removed his jacket and placed it over her shoulders to help keep her warm.

"Laura, I'm sorry if what I said back there made you uncomfortable. You know I don't think these things through. I know I'm selfish. I just say what's on my mind."

Laura pulled the jacket lapels closed and said, "It didn't embarrass me. It just surprised me a bit. This whole thing has been kind of a shock. I came down here figuring I'd have to fight off all these guys' advances. Then I run into you and I let my defenses down."

"Hey, wait a minute. I wasn't trying to hit on you."

Laura thought for a second and then replied, "That isn't it. You weren't out of line at all."

"So what's got you puzzling now?"

Laura reached over, took Josh's hand in hers, and said, "Maybe I'm disappointed you didn't try to hit on me."

Josh stopped in his tracks and pulled on Laura's hand. She turned to him and in the arched walkway leading down to her room, they stood face to face. "What are you saying?" he asked.

"Over dinner, reminiscing about old times, a lot of those old feelings came back to me too. I kept hoping you were married or something, so I could keep the defenses up and avoid facing what I feel."

Laura reached around Josh, who was still a bit in shock at what he was hearing, and pulled herself up against his chest. In her heels, she was almost exactly his height. She continued with, "After so many years of empty promises and hollow offers from men I couldn't trust, I end up here, unexpectedly in the arms of the last man I trusted."

"Are you afraid of what might happen if you say yes?"

Laura put her lips very close to his and said, "No. I'm afraid of what I might miss if I decide to say no."

Josh took her words as his cue to make his move. He reached up and cupped his hands around her face, pausing briefly before pulling her lips to his. All the barriers were down and all the old feelings they had been holding back came rushing out.

There was a mutual hunger to their kiss and a sense of desperation in their embrace. Pressed firmly against each other's body, they bounced off one wall and then the other as they struggled to walk their way to the door of Laura's room.

Josh accidentally nipped her tongue when he reacted to the doorknob jabbing in his back when he fell against the door. Refusing to stop their frenzied and probing kisses, Laura fumbled to find the keys to the room. They kept shifting back and forth, blindly trying to aim the key into the lock. Finally, she managed to unlock the door and it gave way under the pressure of their bodies.

The door slammed against the wall as they fell into the room and onto the bed. The light from outside, briefly lit the room like a flashbulb, but it just as quickly darkened as the door rebounded from the wall and slammed shut. The only remaining light filtered into the room through the very sheer drapes covering the partially closed plantation shutters in the window. The shadows of the louvers cast stripes across the wall, the bed, and their lusting bodies.

They fell to the bed with Laura on top of Josh. She broke their impassioned kisses just long enough to raise her body, toss his coat from her shoulders, and swing it above her head like a lasso before throwing it into the corner. Laura tossed her hair briefly and then dove back onto Josh, locking lips and probing deeply with her tongue.

They pawed desperately at each other's bodies, grabbing at whatever limb or joint they could find to pull themselves closer together. Josh reached down with both hands and grabbed at Laura's hips, cradling one cheek of her buttocks in each hand. Through the fabric of her flowing skirt, he could feel the firmness of her flesh and the fact she was wearing a garter belt instead of pantyhose. Not that he needed any help, but this detail fueled his passion more and strengthened the urgency of his desire to have her.

Laura worked both of her hands between them and up to Josh's chest. Doing a small push-up with her arms, she grabbed the lapels of his open shirt and violently pulled them apart. Fabric ripped and buttons flew. As her hands spread apart, it left nothing to support her and she fell back onto Josh's now bare chest. Through the thin material of her blouse, she could feel the soft bristles of his chest hair tickling her skin.

The frantic couple were not wholly on the bed. Their feet were still in contact with the floor and both desperately tried to propel their bodies further up onto the bed. As they gained distance, Josh used his toes, one at a time, to push his shoes off his feet. The first fell to the floor with a thump, but the second gained extra momentum from the bouncing bed and flew into the air, rebounding off the lamp on the night stand.

Laura flinched as the shoe crashed into the lamp, but she was having a different problem with her shoes. The strap on her open back shoes made it impossible for her to just flick them off with her feet. She had to lift each leg up behind her and then reach back to pull the strap free and remove the shoe and toss it aside. Each time she reached for her foot, the change in support and her center of gravity, caused her belly and hips to grind harder into Josh's body and the growing bulk of his manhood.

Between panting pauses to catch their breath, Josh returned her previous favor and ripped open Laura's blouse. In the diminished light he could clearly see the lacy push-up bra she was wearing underneath. As she fell back onto his chest, the bra's effect was enhanced by the pressure of their chests pressing against each other as Laura wiggled out of her sleeves. For a moment he thought the velvet mounds were going to pop out of their cups and into his face.

When they didn't, Josh decided to pull Laura up enough to bury his face between them. He felt their warmth mold themselves around his face as he slowly rolled his face from side to side. Laura did not resist and even helped by pushing on each breast's outboard side with her hands. Eventually, he could no longer breathe and he had to lift her off of him slightly.

Josh realized the bra closed in the front, and although he tried, he could not figure out how to open it. Laura slid her knees up along side him so she could sit on top of him. As she rose, she panted out, "Here. Let me help you with it."

Relieved of their support and returned to the effect of gravity, Laura's breasts swung down and out, bouncing briefly before settling into their normal position. She heard Josh sigh at the vision, so she cradled them in her hands for a second, let them bounce again, and then asked him, "Do you like what you see?"

He swallowed back a groan and said, "Baby, you know I do."

The lovers shifted their weight and swung around to let Laura sit on the bed and Josh to sit up in front of her. They took each other in their arms for a long embrace, before Laura let go and fell back onto the bed. While he watched, she unbuttoned the wrap portion of her skirt, slid it down off her hips, and tossed it off the bed.

Josh paused to look at her. The white garter belt, white panties, and the white, lace topped, thigh-high hose were an interesting contrast against her suntanned skin. It was made even more erotic by the striped shadows cast across her body by the shutter slats in the window. He removed his shirt, threw it aside, and fell on her in a full body embrace.

Laura reached up behind him to the belt of his slacks. As she ran her fingers along the border, she came to the butt end of his revolver, carried in an inside-the-pants holster in the small of his back. She thought about pulling it out to tease him, but thought better of it.

Instead, she continued along to the small leather pouch in which he carried his handcuffs. Laura quickly undid the snap flap and fished the cuffs out with one finger. She held them over her head to him and asked, "What should we do with these?"

Josh's first reaction was one of a man having his pocket picked and just finding out. He reached for the pouch and found it empty, then he looked into her eyes and saw the impish smile on her face. He sat up and took the handcuffs off her finger. Laura held out her hands and said, "What have I done, officer?"

Josh quickly slapped one cuff on her wrist and then without much resistance from Laura, he pulled her hands backward to handcuff her other wrist around one of the uprights in the bed's headboard. Josh stood up and said threateningly, "You're going to tell me where you hid the drugs, even if I have to beat it out of you."

"No way, man. There's no way I'm going to tell you. I'd tell you to search me if you had the nerve, but as you can see there's really no where for me to hide the drugs."

Josh slipped the belt out from the belt loops around his trousers waistband and started to run the tip of the leather up and down Laura's legs. Suddenly he flicked the end of it hard onto the meaty part of her bare thighs, just above the hose, with a nice "snap" and then said, “Listen to me, bitch! You've still got a couple of places I could look, so I'll give you one more chance. Do we do this the easy way or the hard way?”

Laura raised herself up slightly, spit at him, and said, “Let's do it the hard way. The really hard way.”

Josh opened his pants and let them fall to the floor. Laura pretended to be afraid of him when he took off his underwear and socks. Josh kept the belt in his hand, stroking the end of it up and down her body. With one finger on his other hand, he started probing the inner recesses of her thighs. He leaned over her and blew air across the rounded bulge under her now moist panties.

She cooed to him, “I didn't hide the drugs up there.”

Josh snapped the end of the leather belt onto her belly and hissed, “Shut up bitch. You had your chance to cooperate. I'll look anywhere I want.” With that, he took the tiny panties and ripped them off her and threw them into one of the piles of clothes strewn around the room.

Josh climbed onto the bed, spread Laura's legs, and knelt between her knees, facing her. He bent over and kissed her bushy mound. Josh flicked a tongue quickly into the milky slit and across her clitoris, making Laura jump in quivered pleasure. “Find anything?” she asked gamely.

Josh snapped the belt on her thigh again. He hit her harder this time. Not hard enough to be painful, but hard enough to leave a lingering tingle and a slight redness to her skin. “I'm still looking,” he replied.

Josh probed her with his tongue, slipping in and out of her labia, and flicking quickly around and across her clitoris. Moisture seemed to be flowing out of her as her excitement grew. Laura couldn't help but move and grind her pelvis into his face. Josh lifted his face and wiped the dew from his chin. He looked at Laura, her eyes still closed from the pleasure he was bringing her. He waited until she opened her eyes before saying, "I haven't been able to find anything yet. I need to bring in a better probing tool."

Josh moved forward and placed the head of his penis against Laura's labia. Laura was so wet and her body so hungry for him, it took no effort for him to enter her. Her body pulled him inside slowly, each contraction of her muscles pulling him in a bit more until he was fully inserted. Having forgotten his role for a moment, he pulled almost all of the way out and slammed his rod home with full force. Laura gasped slightly, not from pain but from the satisfying waves of pleasure sweeping across her body.

Josh pulled out again and slowly forced himself in as far as he could possibly go and then whispered into her ear, "I think I found what I was looking for."

Much to his surprise, Laura's arms wrapped around his neck and shoulders. One of the cuffs dangled open from its chain on one of her wrists. "I think I found what I was looking for too," she replied.

"How in the hell..."

Laura's chuckle interrupted him as she said, "I've always kept an extra handcuff key on the charm bracelet I wear. You never know where or when you'll need it."

With everything out on the table now, they settled into a slower more satisfying rhythm to their passion. Laura lost herself in the feelings building inside her as she neared orgasm. She clawed at Josh's back, not hard enough to draw blood, but enough to leave tiny red trails on his skin.

Josh could feel Laura's body tightening in preparation for her release. This added sensation became the last piece in Josh's puzzle and he could no longer contain his own orgasm. Laura arched her back, shoving her pelvis up toward his, two strokes before Josh's spasms began. Laura's breathing became halting and gaspy, while Josh's breathing flowed from flaring nostrils.

In sweaty exhaustion they rolled over on their sides, still desperately clinging to each other. After a few minutes she asked, “Did you ever think police work could be this much fun?”

Josh thought for a second, started to say something and then decided not to respond. A few minutes later he rolled away from her to make it easier for him to breathe. He took Laura's hand in his and squeezed it gently, “I'd forgotten just how wonderful you are.”

Laura sat up and ran her hand through her hair, the handcuffs still dangling from her wrist. They both saw the cuffs and started to laugh. She looked at him and said, “I'll give you a few minutes to recover and then it's my turn to interrogate you.”

Chapter 22

Consciousness slowly returned to Josh's mind, as the bright light of morning began to shine through the window and into the room. Lying on his side, naked, he was facing the window. As he opened his eyes, Josh had to squint and partially block the rays with his hand.

Slowly, he became more aware of his surroundings and he warmly remembered the evening's escapades. Josh also slowly became aware of something moving on his bare butt. He started to roll over to see what was going on when Laura called out from behind him, “Don't move for a second or two.”

“What are you doing?”

"I'm a morning person. You were sleeping so soundly, I went for a quick walk on the beach. I got back and you were still sleeping. I got undressed and crawled back into bed with you."

"That's not what I meant. I wanted to know what you're doing behind me."

"I was getting bored, so I decided to take the ink pen and give you a tattoo on your butt to remember me. There. It's finished."

Josh rolled over and kissed her sweetly before saying, "I don't need a tattoo to remember you."

Laura smacked his butt with her hand and said, "Well, it's too late. You've already got it. So get dressed. I'm hungry and I want breakfast."

"All right," he said. "I wouldn't want you to start pouting."

Josh got out of bed and went into the bathroom to urinate. As he walked by the sink, he saw his reflection in the mirrors on the closet doors. He continued into the bathroom to do his business, but stopped in mid-stream. He ran out of the bathroom and looked hard at the mirrored view.

Josh puzzled a few times, unable to read the reversed writing on his backside. He contorted his body and pulled at his buttock to get a direct view. In a shocked voice, he screamed to Laura, "What the hell is this?"

"I told you. It's a tattoo to remember me by."

"That's not what I meant. Why did you write "banque nationale du paris" on my butt?"

Indignant at his reaction, she said in a huff, "It will wash off in a day or two. I didn't mean to piss you off."

"You're not getting my drift. It was cute of you to draw on my butt. I appreciate what you did. A heart or a flower would have been cute, but I want to know what made you draw this particular tattoo?"

"I don't see what difference it makes. It just popped into my mind. A month or two ago I investigated a murder and the victim had this tattoo on his behind. It's been rattling around in my head since then, so I thought it was funny to see it on you. Why?"

Josh plopped himself down in a chair and said, "You're not going to believe this. I can't believe it."

"Believe what?"

"Months ago, I investigated two murders where the victims had this particular tattoo."

Amazed, Laura asked, "You had two victims with this tattoo?"

"Yeah. Some homosexual got snuffed with a gunshot up the rear and then some time later, a dock worker was squashed by a cargo container. How did yours buy the farm?"

"It wasn't nearly as interesting as yours. It was a pawn shop robbery. The guy was stuffed naked into a safe. Suffocated in there. Why?"

Josh rubbed his face and some of the sleep from his eyes before saying, "Hell. My guys have been giving me grief because I blew them off about the coincidence. They wanted me to call Paris and ask about the tattoo. I told them to take a hike."

"Don't blame yourself," Laura said. "I didn't think anything about the one I had. It never crossed my mind to do anything else with it but ask around at the tattoo parlors. What do you think we should do now?"

"Damned if I know. Is there any chance I can get a look at your crime scene photos?"

"You want me to send them to you in Frisco?"

Josh reacted emphatically, "No! The last thing I need is to have my office telling me they told me so."

Laura wondered, "So what do you want to do?"

"I had already scheduled a couple of extra days off to spend down here. I suppose I could drive up to Los Angeles and get a look before I fly back to Frisco."

Laura thought about it for a second, grinned slyly, and said, "I've got an even better idea. Come spend those extra days with me."

"Wouldn't it be considered moving a bit too fast?"

"I don't care," she declared. "It's not like we'll do anything, and I mean anything, we didn't already do last night."

Josh tried to cover his mistake with, "I just wanted to be sure what we're talking about. We've sort of been down this road before."

"Okay. Would it make you feel any better if I said I just wanted to be in on the action?"

"Maybe. Why?"

"It was my first solo murder case. Besides, it was my artwork which triggered you to make the connection. I deserve part of the collar."

Josh liked her nerve and professional desire. He laughed a bit and asked, "Where should I stay?"

"You know damn well you're staying with me. I'll consider it a fringe benefit of the job."

Josh looked at the clock, then started putting on his clothes. "Where are you going?" asked Laura.

"In case you forgot, this is not my room."

"Oh yeah."

"Laura. You order up breakfast from room service. I'll go back to my room, get cleaned up, and come back here. We've still got the next two days of this meeting to get through."

Laura stood up and walked over to Josh, showing off her naked body. She curled her index finger in the hair on his chest and cooed, "We've also got the next two nights of this convention to get through."

Chapter 23

Heads in the Homicide office turned as Laura Miles slammed down the receiver of the telephone and screamed, "Au revoir my ass!"

"Strike out again?" asked Josh.

Laura picked up a pencil and snapped it into two pieces with her hands. "Pompous, self-righteous son of a bitch. I'd always heard the French were rude, but give it a rest."

Josh shook his head a moment and then asked, "So what did they say?"

Over-exaggerating a French accent she said, "We are so sorry mademoiselle, but we can not give out zee information you require."

"Wouldn't they even tell you why anyone would have a tattoo with their bank's name on their butt?"

"They claim to know nothing about it and even if they did, it is against their policy to give out the information."

The two of them sat silently looking at each other. After a few seconds, they both broke out laughing. Josh was the first to resume the conversation. He held up the manila folder of crime scene photos and asked, "Was there any indication of a robbery at this pawn shop?"

"Robbery doesn't seem to be the motive," she said. "There was a stash of cash taken, but a ton of jewelry was left almost untouched."

"What do you mean almost untouched?"

Laura reached across the desks and pawed through the photos until she found the one she wanted. She pointed to the case and said, "Apparently the robber looked through the jewelry, but they returned everything to the case. The owner's accountant knew the layout. He confirmed nothing was taken, but that the jewelry was rearranged."

"Strange," said Josh as the telephone on the desk rang.

"Homicide. Detective Miles. Uh-huh. What? Where? Are you sure? I'll be right there."

Josh sat up and asked, "What was that all about?"

"You're not going to believe this. We've got another murder and the victim's got a tattoo on their butt."

Simultaneously they grabbed their coats. Josh scooped up the photo file of the pawn shop murder scene and opened the door for Laura as they headed down the hall to the parking lot. They came out the back door of the building into the sunlight, and both automatically threw on their sunglasses. They got to Laura's car and jumped inside. "How far away is it?" asked Josh.

As she turned the key, Laura replied, "Fifteen or twenty minutes. It's up near Hollywood."

Even though he wasn't driving, Josh looked both ways as they pulled out of the parking lot and onto the street. As they hit the freeway entrance, Josh inquired, "So what do we know about the victim?"

"He's some plastic surgeon. That's all I know."

There were a few seconds of silence as they drove down the road. Josh said, "I called my people and they're sending down copies of my files so we can compare notes."

"Did you ask them about hanging on in Los Angeles for a while?"

"Yeah, I did and they weren't thrilled about it. They told me no, but if this one turns out to be linked to it, they're going to have to let me stay."

Laura thought for a second, smiled at Josh and said, "That would be convenient."

Josh could not prevent a sly and silly grin from spreading over his face as he said, "Yeah, well, it makes sense too."

Laura thought and then cautiously asked, "Josh, do you think we need to call the FBI in on this?"

"No way. This one is ours. Even if we wanted to, they probably wouldn't step in. The killer hasn't crossed state lines yet."

"I know that. What I was asking, was whether or not we should share this with them, so they can see if there's been any other killings around the country."

Josh thought about it for a second or two and then said, "Let's sit on it for a bit. At least until we see if we can put this together ourselves. We can always call them in."

Laura suggested, "Why don't we at least put a description of the tattoo out over the teletype? Maybe this person has killed before and like us, there are other departments who didn't know what to make of the tattoo."

"That sounds like a good idea, as long as you put your name on it. I don't want to advertise to every police department in the country I'm looking for dead men with tattoos on their butt."

Laura exited the freeway and turned onto surface streets. When she found the correct street and resumed a stable course, she asked, "What do you make of these tattoos?"

"Hell if I know. I didn't think about it when I had two of my own. When we get all of the records together and compare notes, maybe something will jump out at us." Josh looked at some of the buildings they were passing, whistled and said, "Wow. There's some serious money around here."

They pulled into the parking lot of a medical building, found a place to park, and shut off the car. As they got out of the car, Laura peered over the roof at the building and said, "Yeah, but apparently money doesn't stop you from getting killed."

Together they entered the office building and took the elevator up to the appropriate floor. They were surprised at the scarcity of police units and activity in the lobby. When the elevator doors opened, the scene was more what they were used to. They fought their way through the police officers who were asking questions of employees. When they got to the door of the doctor's office, Laura found her boss, Lieutenant Baker, waiting for them.

"Laura. How you doing?" he asked.

"Just fine, lieutenant."

Baker said, "Well, Johnson and Wiley originally got the call, but as soon as they saw the tattoo, we figured we'd better get you involved."

"Lieutenant. You remember Inspector Dunbar from the San Francisco police department, don't you?"

The two men shook hands and Baker said, "Yes. I met you this morning at the precinct house. I seem to recall you've had a couple of these murders up your way, haven't you?"

"Yes sir. Two men. They had the same tattoo as the pawnshop owner you guys found."

"Damnedest thing I've every seen." Baker turned to Laura and continued with, "So, Detective Miles, where do you want to begin?"

Feeling like she was being graded by a teacher, she asked him, "What do we know so far?"

Baker said, "Well, I think we've got what you'd consider your everyday Hollywood plastic surgeon. Doctor's name is Fletcher, Peter Fletcher."

"What do we know about him?" inquired Laura.

"Victim's in his forties, six feet tall, about 180 pounds, with blue eyes and blond hair. His employees told us he'd never been married. According to them, he prefers the free life, dating his more famous patients whenever possible."

Dunbar broke in asking, "Are you insinuating one of his disgruntled patients or a jealous husband may have snuffed him?"

"No, not really, but it is a possibility."

"Who found the body?" asked detective Miles.

"When the office staff came in this morning, they found the body. The last time they saw the doctor was on Friday night. No one was in the office Saturday or yesterday, so we can assume the murder took place some time over the weekend."

Dunbar asked, "Who saw him last on Friday?"

"One of the nurses. She said he stayed late to finish some paperwork. She went home and that's the last anyone saw of him."

Laura thought for a second and then asked, "Did the nurse say anything to the doctor before she left?"

"Very good question, detective," smiled the lieutenant. "The nurse asked the doctor what he was doing and the doctor said he was going to work on some paperwork until eight when he had a hot date waiting."

Laura added, "Did she lock up?"

"Yes she did. They locked the front office doors at six. The office staff leaves through a side door which locks behind them as they leave."

Josh wanted to know, "Were there any signs of forced entry?"

"Nothing. Someone either had a key or the doctor let them in."

"Not necessarily, lieutenant," said Laura. "The killer could have been waiting in the hall. When someone left, they could have slipped in before the door finished closing."

"Not a bad idea," said Baker, "but we already asked about it. The nurses say the door opens into a big hallway. They would have seen anyone who was waiting to slip in."

"The killer could have hidden in the office, earlier in the day, and waited until everyone left."

Baker looked at Dunbar and then said, "Yes, I suppose they could have."

Laura wanted to know, "What was the method of murder?"

Lieutenant Baker smiled, chuckled, and then said, "I've been waiting for you to ask that. I can't tell you."

Laura had an edge to her voice when she asked, "What do you mean, you can't tell us?"

"I could tell you, but you'd never believe me. You've really got to see this yourself."

The trio walked into the waiting area of the doctor's office. Baker told everyone to leave for a while. Laura wanted to know, "Why are you chasing everyone out?"

Baker said, "I know you're tough, but this one is a real peach. For your sake, I chased everyone out. If you can't handle it, I didn't want to embarrass you."

Indignant, she said, "If you can handle this, I can handle it."

"Okay. As you wish." Having said that, Baker opened the door to one of the rooms the doctor used for in-office surgeries. As the door swung open, he bowed and gestured with his arm for them to enter. "I hope you're ready. This is a real doozy."

Josh and Laura walked into the brightly lit room to find Dr. Fletcher lying on the operating table. The table was tilted at about thirty degrees, with the head up. The two arm boards of the operating table were extended in such a way as to create the appearance of a make-shift cross.

"What in the hell happened?" asked Josh.

Laura looked at the body and winced, but not wanting to admit to the boss the weakness in her knees, Laura steeled herself to the image before her eyes. Laura felt her strength returning and she was finally able to get into the "clinical" mentality homicide investigators develop.

This state of mind is best described as a morbid curiosity. The victim becomes impersonal, an object to examine and analyze, like studying a mummy. The initial shock of the horror, caught her off-guard. Trying to sound tough, she said, "What ever happened took time. The killer certainly was not in a hurry."

The victim was naked and strapped to the table so he would not slide off onto the floor. The doctor's body parts had been surgically re-arranged. It was not his arms which were strapped to the arm boards of the table, but his legs. Sliced off at the hip, each leg was sutured with large, thick black stitches to the shoulder.

The arms were similarly removed at the shoulder and sewn on at the hips. The head had been severed and turned around halfway, reattached to the torso so the head looked over the man's back. The torso and attached limbs were on the table in such a manner that the doctor faced the viewer and his buttocks were clearly aimed at you.

The most intriguing feature of the corpse was the man's penis. For some unknown reason, the penis had been removed and stitched onto the doctor's chin. Dangling there it had the slight appearance of an elephant's trunk. This became the one item which drew the trio's attention most. They slowly walked over to the body. Baker stood directly in front of the body. Laura walked around to one side, while Josh walked around to the other. At almost the same time, the three leaned in to get a closer look.

Baker asked, "Have you ever seen anything so weird?"

Josh whispered, "Why in the hell would anyone do this?"

Laura, in an attempt to sound in control of her feelings, smiled and said, "Oh, I don't know. Personally, I think that's where God should have put it in the first place."

Chapter 24

Josh Dunbar opened the meeting with, "Okay, folks. You've all had a chance over the past ten days to go over the material again. Doing this meeting over the telephone gets a bit tricky, so let's see if we can be productive. Something besides the damned tattoo connects these four men. I want to find out what it is. Any ideas?"

The meeting was being held in the LAPD office of Lieutenant Baker. His telephone speaker/microphone unit sat in the middle of his desk, while a dozen investigators, technicians, Josh, and Laura sat in a haphazard circle around the desk. The phone line was connected to a similar gathering in San Francisco. After Josh's ill-designed question, a dozen voices tried to talk all at once.

Josh kept repeating himself until everyone shut up. "Hey! Hey! Will you all...hey...would you just shut up. Okay. That one was my fault. We can't all speak at once. Del? Are you there?"

"Yeah, partner. What do you need?"

"Have we been able to find anything in their past to link them up?"

You could hear Delano rustling paper during the pause before he said, "Not much. They were all about the same age. They were born in different parts, all over the country. The Cummings guy and the pawnshop owner were locals. The doctor was born in Alabama. We're not really sure where the faggot was born, but he grew up in New York and then Las Vegas."

Laura wanted to know, "What about schools?"

"Nothing there. Two just barely finished high school, one didn't, and the other was the doctor."

A Los Angeles detective came into the room, a file in his hand, just in time to hear the last question and answer. He chimed in with, "I may have something here. These four guys all served in Europe during World War II."

Josh sat up in his chair saying, "Now there's some help. Did they serve in the same outfit?"

"We're still trying to get those records from the Army. At the end of the war they were stationed in France, cleaning up after the German retreat. We know they served in the same infantry division, but it will be a while before we know if they served in the same unit."

Laura smiled, as it was one of her people who turned up the clues. Patting him on the back, she said to the officer, "Way to go."

"Okay," said Josh. "So, we've got these four guys in the war. Is there anything else to tie them together? Was there anything at their home, you know, letters, photographs, that kind of thing?"

Del spoke first, "There was nothing at the fairy's place except theater posters and frilly costumes. The dock worker's house had a scrap book from the war. There really wasn't much in it. A couple of medals, uniform patches, you know what I mean." Del paused for a second and then you could hear more paper rustling just before he continued with, "Now that I think about it, there were some letters, newsletter kind of things."

"What are you saying?" asked Josh.

Del replied, "Yeah. Here it is. There were two issues of something called 'Here's To Your Health' lying on the dresser in his bedroom. At first I didn't think anything of it, but there were two drawings on the headline of the paper. One was an Army insignia for the 7th Infantry. The other was some drinking glass, you know, like a big goblet."

All of a sudden, one of the Los Angeles technicians started rifling through a stack of photographs. Most fell onto the floor, but then he suddenly held one up in the air toward Josh and said, "Ask him if it looked anything like this?"

Laura stood and leaned over to get a look at the photo with Josh. Laura asked, "Where'd this turn up?"

The technician was trying to pick up the pile of paper he'd dropped, while still answering, "We found a couple of these in the doctor's office, on his desk to be exact. We didn't think much of it, after all, it was a doctor's office. We just thought it was some medical literature."

"All right. Now, we're getting somewhere," said Josh as he rubbed his hands together. "I think this is probably our best bet for now. I need everyone to get back out to the crime scenes, the victims' homes and apartments, and look for those newsletters. Find out who is publishing this thing."

Laura did not want Josh hogging all the limelight. She jumped in with, "And while you're at it, go through all their photo albums. Look for pictures from the war. Go through their mail. Maybe they kept in touch with some of their old war buddies. Something other than murder ties these four together. Let's find it."

Dunbar took over and said, "If no one has any questions in San Francisco, let's hit the street." There was no reply on the telephone speaker other than the shuffling of chair legs on linoleum floors and the click of the receiver being put down.

The office in Los Angeles was just about to break up as well, when a clerk came into the room holding a teletype printout. Everyone froze in their tracks with curiosity as the clerk said, "Detective Miles. This just came in for you. It's a reply to your broadcast message."

Laura grabbed the paper and began to read. Many of the men tried to read over her shoulder, but most were not tall enough or were in a bad position to see the paper. "What does it say?" asked Lt. Baker.

Laura said, "There's been another murder of a man with the same tattoo. This one is in Sweetwater, Oklahoma."

Josh asked, "When did it happen?"

"Yesterday. Happened at a rodeo."

"How was the guy murdered?"

"This doesn't say. It just says the victim had a tattoo which matched our description. Nothing else."

Lt. Baker took charge, "You all know what you're supposed to do, so let's get going. Hit those two crime scenes and see what you can turn up. Miles and Dunbar, you stay here. The rest of you, get going!"

When the room emptied, Baker closed the door behind the crowd and said to the other two, "That cuts it! Call the FBI. I wanted to break this ourselves as much as you two did, but we've crossed state lines. If we don't call them in now, there'll be hell to pay later."

Laura wanted to know, "Do you think they'll let us stay involved?"

Josh was the first to answer. He said, "Oh, yeah. They'll let us stay involved. I've dealt with them before. They like to come in and take over, but they make a big deal of making it a joint effort. As far as I'm concerned, they want to take all the credit if it goes right, and leave us to blame if it goes wrong."

Baker started to correct Dunbar, but then softened a bit when he said, "Look. Normally, I'd have chewed your butt for such an attitude, but I can't say I don't agree with you. We've had to deal with the FBI a few times ourselves."

Dunbar quipped, "Yeah. It isn't a fun experience."

"Unfortunately, we've got no choice. We've got to call them."

Detective Miles inquired, "This is a two way street isn't it? I mean, if we share our information with them, they've got to share theirs with us don't they?"

Dunbar bit off the end of a fingernail, spit it out in disgust, saying, "That's the way it is supposed to work, but it doesn't generally happen that way."

Baker agreed, "Let's not take any chances. Dunbar, your boss cleared you to work with us as long as necessary to solve these cases. Laura, you stay on this as well. I'm less interested in whether LA or Frisco gets the murderer first, than I am in seeing one of us keeps the credit from going to the Feds."

Laura asked, "So what do you want us to do?"

"When the FBI shows up here, tell them only what they ask for. Take it slow and don't offer anything extra until they agree to keep one or both of you firmly involved. I want us there for the collar instead of reading about it in the paper one morning."

Laura nodded and asked, "What are you going to do, boss?"

"I'm going to go place the call to the FBI. I know the local office director. Maybe I can at least get it assigned to a local agent and not some hot shot out of the Washington Bureau."

Chapter 25

The back of Lt. Baker's office butted against one of the building's outside walls. A small window provided most of the light in the room, although the smoggy air of Los Angeles gave the light a sickly yellow tint Three walls of his office were wood, from a standing person's waist to the floor, and glass from the waist to the ceiling. Venetian blinds in varying degrees of being open, covered the glass.

Detective Miles and Inspector Dunbar sat in the office watching the different categories of people stream by. Some looked in at them out of curiosity, while others, mostly in handcuffs, looked at them in disdain. Josh and Laura were waiting for Lt. Baker to finish his phone call. When he hung up the phone, Laura asked, "So, do they finally have the case assigned to someone? It's been three damned days."

"As a matter of fact, they do," replied her boss. "They've assigned it to some guy named Sinclair. Special Agent Lewis Sinclair."

Detective Miles reacted to the name, causing her boss to ask, "What's up? Do you know him?"

"Yes, I do. We worked together a few years ago. Don't you remember? It was the, uh, the uh, Cardinal Bank deal."

"Oh yeah, the case where the bank manager was laundering drug and prostitution money through their out-of-state branches. Was that the guy? Damn."

Josh wanted know, "Why the reaction?"

Laura filled in the details with, "The guy's a weasel. He's so clean he squeaks. Just the type the FBI loves to fast track. We did all of the legwork and he took all of the glory. I think he got a promotion out of it."

"And we got squat," added Baker.

Josh observed, "Well, at least we don't have to think twice about whether we openly share information with him."

Baker eased forward in his chair, intertwined the fingers of his hands, and said, "He'll be here in fifteen minutes and he's bringing the photos from the crime scene in Oklahoma. Now, where are we with the newsletter thing?"

Josh pulled out a notebook. "The newsletter had a name and address for a Jerome Miller of New York City. It requested that anyone who wanted to contribute material or information should write him in New York."

"How often is it published?" asked Laura.

"According to the newsletter, it comes out every six months. By the edition numbers on the banner, it supposedly has been printed since 1950."

"Did you call this Jerome Miller?" inquired Baker.

"I called him yesterday. When I told him I was a cop, he clammed up. He didn't seem too cooperative until I told him about the murders."

Laura asked, "After he heard, did he loosen up a bit?"

"No, exactly the opposite. He answered my questions okay, but he had this evasive tone to his voice, sort of like he was hiding something."

"Okay, so the guy was shook up from the news. What did he tell you?" asked a bored lieutenant.

"When I asked him about the newsletter, he had no problem with it. He told me that a bunch of guys he served with in the war made it up to stay in touch over the years. He mentioned they recently had a twentieth reunion."

Laura asked him, "Was he willing to give you a list of their names?"

"He even gave me their addresses. Apparently, sharing this information isn't a problem for him. Besides our five victims, there is this Miller guy and four others. There's two guys from New York named Williams and Carletti. There's one guy in Chicago and another in Iowa."

Laura reminded the two men, "That still doesn't really explain the connection. Did you ask him why anyone would want to kill them?"

"When I asked the question, this guy's blood must of gone ice cold. He went stone cold silent for a good minute, and then told me he didn't know any reason why anyone would be after them."

Baker asked, "Did you believe him?"

"Not for a minute. He's hiding something."

The telephone on Baker's desk rang. He picked it up saying, "Yeah. Okay. Send him up." Baker returned the handset to the phone's cradle and said, "Sinclair is here. Let's remember to keep things close to the vest until we're forced to tell him anything. Don't block the investigation, but don't give everything away. I want us firmly in on the deal, every step of the way, before we open up. Got it?"

Laura and Josh nodded. There was a rap at the closed door to Baker's office. Laura was facing the door enough that she needed only to look up. Josh had to turn around in his chair. He took one look at the FBI agent and whistled, "Whoa! He could be a recruiting poster-boy for the FBI"

Baker motioned the agent into the office. As the door swung open and he walked in, the three officers sat silently, staring at the agent. The agent was wearing a perfectly tailored blue suit, white shirt, and a striped tie. His shoes were perfectly shined. Over his left arm was draped a neatly folded, almost unwrinkled trench coat, and in his hand he carried a perfectly creased fedora. He carried a brown valise in his right hand. Putting it down, he reached out to Baker and said, “Special Agent Lewis Sinclair. Nice to see you again Lieutenant Baker.”

Baker shook the agent's hand and then motioned to the other two officers, “This is Inspector Josh Dunbar of the San Francisco Police Department. He's on loan to us for a while.”

“Nice to meet you Inspector.”

Still a bit stunned at the agent's appearance, Josh hesitated and then stood to shake the man's hand. Baker motioned to Laura and said, “And this is Detective Laura Miles. Do you remember her?”

The FBI agent put his coat over the arm of a chair, reached across for Laura's hand, and instead of shaking it, he brought it up to his lips and said, “How could I forget her?” He started to kiss the back of her hand, but she pulled her hand away, somewhat embarrassed.

“I'm sorry,” said Sinclair. “I apologize. You see, I've just returned from serving in Paris for a year. I was sharing our investigative techniques with the French. In France, kissing a beautiful woman's hand is an accepted greeting. I must have forgotten where I was for a moment.”

Laura acknowledged the apology and then asked, “Is that why they assigned the case to you?”

“Yes. That was one of the many reasons. The bureau thought my connections in France might come in handy. In fact, I understand you tried to call the National Bank of Paris regarding the tattoo. Did you get any information?”

“No. The rude bastards wouldn't tell me anything,” grumbled Detective Miles.

“I'm not surprised. It sometimes takes a certain level of sophistication, to get cooperation from the French."

Dunbar was getting fed up with the agent's pompous airs. “Are you saying you're better than us?”

Ignoring the comment, the FBI agent picked up his briefcase, opened the latch and pulled out a file. He placed it on the desk and said, "Here are the files and photos from the murder in Oklahoma. While you look them over, I'll see what I can find out from Paris."

The agent looked at his watch, pulled out a small telephone book from his jacket pocket, and said, "Let's see, it is about eight here and Paris is nine hours ahead of us. That makes it five in the evening there. The bank is probably closed, but I have a private phone number for the president of the bank. Lieutenant, is there a telephone I might use?"

Laura and Josh grabbed the file. When the FBI agent wasn't looking, they both made obscene gestures about his attitude. In the background, they could hear him jabbering away in French on the telephone with someone. While he talked, they opened the file.

"Geesh. Get a look at this," said Josh. "This guy looks like a ball of raw meat."

The three officers were still pouring over the photos and reports when Special Agent Sinclair concluded his phone call. He came over to the trio and said, "Thankfully, Jacques was still in his office."

Baker asked, "Were you able to find out anything?"

"Not as much as you might like, but given what we are dealing with here, I'd say I did pretty well."

Josh was impatient when he asked, "Okay. So what did you find out?"

The FBI agent sat down, crossed his legs, and casually said, "We are dealing with a 'tontine'."

Everyone sat for a second, staring at each other. Finally Laura asked, "What is a tontine?"

Enjoying his position of superiority in this matter, the agent said, "Actually, it's quite fascinating. A tontine is an agreement or contract, between several people. It started toward the end of the middle ages, actually. It wasn't until the Renaissance, in Italy, that it became popular. Eventually, it became firmly entrenched as part of French honor and tradition."

Josh felt he was being brushed off with the answer, so he pressed the agent with, "Hold your emotions back, bud, and skip the history lesson. Give it to me one more time, but in language a simple man like me can understand."

"When there is a dispute in ownership for something valuable, a group of individuals can agree to a tontine to resolve the dispute. The last person in the group alive, gets the prize."

Baker leaned back in his chair and put his hands behind his head. "So you are implying the ten guys we're talking about have entered into this tontine thing?"

Trying to stop him, Josh and Laura reacted to Baker's slip up by waving their hands. Unfortunately, Sinclair had already caught on to the information and asked, "What ten men are you talking about lieutenant?"

Realizing he made a mistake, he admitted, "Before you got here, we were able to find out something which connects the murders. It seems ten men served together in World War II and have stayed in touch through a newsletter one of them prints. We think they all have the tattoos."

Sinclair thought about it for a second, knowing information was being controlled. He said, "That would make sense. According to the bank, there is a record of a tontine on file with a group of American soldiers. The records indicate that all the parties involved have these tattoos."

Josh wanted to know, "Why would they have the bank's name on a tattoo?"

"I would guess they thought there was a good chance of them getting killed in action before the war was over. If a Frenchman found the body, he'd report it to the bank and they would record the death for the records."

"Did this banker tell you how many men and their names?" asked Baker.

The FBI agent chuckled and said, "No. You don't understand the seriousness of a tontine. The French consider their honor as important as eating and breathing. Particularly in the old days. If you insulted the honor of a Frenchman, he would kill you on the spot or challenge you to a duel. French society accepted these things and in many cases, created elaborate rules to protect them. The records of a tontine are protected with the highest secrecy."

Josh was frustrated with the facts and irritated with the agent's arrogant attitude when he asked, "Are you saying they would deliberately withhold information on a murder investigation?"

"Again, you miss the subtlety of the point. The only thing which matters to the bank, is fulfilling their obligation on the tontine. They don't care under what circumstances the men die. They only record the deaths and give the valuables to the last survivor."

"Would this friend of yours tell you what the last survivor gets?" wondered Laura.

"Of all of the things they protect, the identity of the subject for the tontine is the most sacred. Even if they knew, the bank would never divulge it."

Baker demanded, "And why in hell wouldn't they?"

The agent shifted in his chair to face the lieutenant directly. "There is both a practical reason and an ethical reason. Ethically, this is tied to the rules of honor governing a tontine. If the bank were to give out this information, they would never be trusted with these matters again. Their reputation would be shot."

"So, what is the practical reason?" asked Dunbar.

"Again, we have to go back to the old days when French society was more chaotic than it is today. There were wars, plagues, Napoleon, and countless revolutionary attempts. To protect fortunes and property, families or conspirators would enter into tontines to both secure their futures and hide their alliances. If the information in tontines were given out freely, men would be killed to get their fortunes or gain power."

Lieutenant Baker thought for a few moments and then asked, "Since they won't tell us for sure, what do you think this valuable item is?"

"It could be anything, or nothing."

Josh's anger and frustration showed as he snapped, "What kind of an answer is that? Anything or nothing. What the hell do you mean by it?"

"The bank could be holding something of only sentimental value, say like a bottle of wine for a last toast to lost comrades. On the other hand, the bank could be holding onto property. I've heard of banks controlling entire blocks of a city, managing and collecting rentals, until the property could be turned over to the last survivor. The bank could also be holding onto money, stocks, bonds, or gold. It could literally be anything."

The four police officers sat silent for a minute, realizing this avenue was a dead end for the time being. Baker picked up the crime file from Oklahoma and said, "Well, apparently we're not going to get anywhere with the bank. We'll just have to lean on one of our currently living participants later. For now, let's review this file."

Sinclair started, "Yes. Fascinating if you ask me. The victim was a rodeo cowboy named Casey Ross. He was found as you see him in the photos, outside the arena in an area where they temporarily keep the horses and bulls. He was found naked, hog tied like a roped calf, and bull whipped to death."

"Sort of a last roundup," commented Josh.

Laura wanted to know, "Why do you consider this fascinating?"

"Almost every square inch of his body was whipped raw and bloody, except where the tattoo was located. The murderer wanted the tattoo to be found."

"Is it particularly significant?" asked Laura.

It was Baker who chimed in with, "It is if you have a personal stake in this tontine thing."

"You are absolutely right," added the FBI agent. "These killings are personal. Very personal. In all five murders, there doesn't seem to have been any struggle prior to the deaths. The killer would have had to get very close to each victim."

Josh stated, "Almost as if they knew them or it was a friend."

"Exactly, Inspector. Except for the dock worker, all of the victims have been found naked. The deaths have all been rather gruesome, you might say, or at least not a simple way to go. No, I think our killer wanted the bodies found and remembered. It also seems apparent they wanted the tattoo discovered so the deaths would be recorded for the tontine."

Baker threw the meeting open to suggestions as to what to do next. Josh was the first one make a suggestion. "I say we start with the guy who writes the newsletter. If anyone knows what's going on, he does."

Sinclair inquired, "I seem to remember you saying there were ten men in this agreement. By my calculation, that still leaves five alive. Do you know who they are?"

Josh and Laura looked at Baker for approval. The lieutenant nodded and Dunbar said, "Yeah. We just found out this morning. There are three men living in New York City, one in Chicago, and another in Iowa."

Sinclair saw the little ritual of getting permission, which further confirmed his suspicion that information to him was being controlled. He asked, "Which one of them prints the newsletter?"

"One of the men in New York."

It was time for Baker to make his play for the team. "I think that's where we need to start. Three out of the five are in New York City. Agent Sinclair, is there any reason why these two officers couldn't accompany you to New York to investigate?"

The agent thought about the situation. The two other officers had information he needed. He could get it, eventually, but it might be helpful to have them along. "No, lieutenant. I can't see any reason at all why they can't be involved. In the spirit of interdepartmental cooperation, I'd love to have them along. The first murders were out here, so I suppose you deserve first shot at prosecuting the murderer."

"Great," said Baker. "Josh and Laura, get your stuff together and fly out to New York..."

"I'm sorry to interrupt you, lieutenant, but as the special agent in charge of this case, I must insist on having complete control. These two fine officers are welcome to participate, but they must report to me. I'm sure you understand."

Realizing he had won one thing and lost another, Baker decided it was best to stay involved at one level rather than not be involved at all. His facial expression fell from joy to resignation as he said, "Yes. I understand. They're under your control. I just want updates from them as we go along."

The FBI agent stood and started to pick up his materials. "Then we're agreed. Detective Miles and

Inspector Dunbar, I'd like you to begin gathering up the materials we'll need to take with us. Then, I want you both to pack for the trip. I will get us booked on a flight tonight. I want us knocking on that guy's door first thing tomorrow morning."

Chapter 26

Four law enforcement officers sat in the living room of the Jew's home, trying to get answers from the reluctant suspect. Laura, Josh, and Lewis had flown all night, getting to New York. Their attention span and bearing were showing the effect of the long night in the air. Josh and Laura's clothing showed the same effect, while strangely, Special Agent Sinclair seemed untouched by the travel. Sitting just as neatly groomed as he had in Los Angeles, Sinclair lead the discussions. The fourth person in the room was the local FBI agent who met them at the airport to drive them around town.

"Okay, Mr. Miller," asked Sinclair, "we've already been down this road a few times this morning and we still aren't any closer to the answers we need. Why won't you tell us what these murders are all about?"

"I told you all I know. Yes, I served in the war with those men, but that was twenty-five years ago. We hardly speak with each other. There were two times when we got together. We had a ten year and a twenty year reunion celebrating the end of the World War. Is it a crime?"

Ignoring the request, Sinclair instead asked the Jew, "We understand you write a newsletter every six months. What's it called?"

"We call it 'Here's To Your Health.' What's wrong with that?"

"Oh, there's nothing wrong with it unless you find it suspicious there are ten names on the mailing list and five of them are now dead. Aren't you the least bit curious as to why?"

"Of course I am, but the whole reason I agreed to do the newsletter was to keep everyone in the group up to date on each other's lives."

"Or deaths?" inquired Inspector Dunbar.

The Jew paused for a second, then replied to Sinclair, "If someone died, I would certainly have written about it, but I also wrote about graduations, birthdays, and vacation trips. That doesn't make me a travel agent."

Sinclair chuckled a bit, maybe a bit punchy from the jet lag. "No, it wouldn't make you a travel agent, but if you look at this our way, you start to look like a murderer."

"I resent the accusation. Why would I want those men dead?"

The three late night travelers looked at each other a second and then Laura asked, "We were hoping you could tell us why someone would want these men dead. You have to admit, it is an interesting connection."

"No offense ma'am, but I'm sure there's quite a few World War veterans who have been killed, who are not on my newsletter mailing list. Do you think I killed them too?"

Josh jumped in with, "Mr. Miller, we are not saying you killed anyone. We're just saying we find it interesting you keep a list of the addresses for all of these men. We thought you could give us some insight into why someone is killing your friends, or at least you might know something else which connects them in some way."

"How many times must I repeat myself? I've told you everything I know."

Sinclair looked over at Laura and gave a prearranged signal. Laura opened a packet of photos and pulled out one. She handed it to the Jew and asked him, "How many World War II veterans have this tattoo on their butt?"

Jerome looked at the enlarged photograph of the tattoo. He could see nothing of who the victim was or the method of death, but there was no denying the officers knew more than they were telling him. The question in the mind of the Jew was how much they knew. He finally whispered, "So you found out about the tattoos, huh?"

"Do you have one of these tattoos?" asked Sinclair.

Jerome looked up from the picture in his hand saying, "You know I do."

"Yes, Mr. Miller. I believe everyone on your list has one. The question is why?"

"You know how servicemen are. We were young and foolish. We wanted something to tie us together, so someone suggested we get tattooed and we did."

Sinclair went on, "Mr. Miller, I've lived in Paris and I can tell you tattoo parlors are hard to find. Soldiers in the Pacific part of the war had no trouble, as tattooing was an island native art. You must have had to look for some time to find an artist to do this."

"Maybe. Maybe we just stumbled on one."

"I find it highly unlikely."

With a belligerent look, Jerome said, "I was there. You weren't."

Sinclair sized up his adversary and continued, "How or where you got the tattoo is really of no concern to me. The bigger question I need answered is why this particular tattoo?"

The Jew looked down at the picture again to buy some time before he had to answer. He thought long and hard before he came up with his answer. "That's part of a funny story actually. We got drunk one night and busted up a little cafe. We got arrested and had to pay for the damages to avoid any criminal charges being filed. We joked about having to take out a loan to pay up and then someone joked about using our butts for collateral. One thing led to another and we got these as the result."

Josh stood and demanded, "You don't expect us to believe bullshit like that do you? Sinclair, get to the point. Ask the son of a bitch about the bank."

Sinclair pointed to the chair Josh had vacated and said, "Sit down Inspector. I'll ask him when I'm ready."

"What are you talking about?" asked the Jew.

Lewis resumed his questioning. "That is a funny story you're telling, Mr. Miller. I suppose it would have been even funnier if I had been there, but it still doesn't answer why someone is trying to kill the men on this list. Is there anything about them you can share with me which might help me understand what's going on?"

"There isn't much to tell. Other than what's already written in the newsletters, I haven't spent much time with any of them since the war."

Sinclair gave another prearranged signal and Laura handed Jerome a group of crime scene photos, each labeled with the victim's name. She asked, "Can you tell us what you remember about each of these men?"

The ploy was planned to loosen his memory and his lips. The officers hoped the shock of the gruesome photos would work. They were close to correct. Jerome flinched at the first one. "We nicknamed this guy Tinker. It was short for Tinkerbell. We knew he was probably a homosexual, but he was a good soldier, someone you could count on in a fight. The army would have thrown him in prison if they knew about his homosexuality, so we kept quiet about it. None of us cared."

Josh said, "Someone apparently cared. They stuffed a gun up his ass and pulled the trigger."

The Jew got squeamish at the description and turned to the next photo. He turned the photo slightly to try and see if it really was the name shown on the photo. Finally he recognized it saying, "Poor Sarge. What happened to him?"

"Someone dropped a huge cargo container on him and squashed him like a bug," explained Josh.

"Hell of a way to go. Sarge was our squad leader. Nice guy at times and tough as nails at others. His heart was in the right place, but there were demons in his head none of us understood." He turned over the next picture. "Moocher? Who would want to murder him?"

Laura asked, "He was suffocated in his own safe. Why did you call him Moocher?"

"Carter could find anything you needed or wanted. You asked and he'd find some way to trade for it. Everyone loved him." Jerome turned to the next one, and almost dropped the photos when he saw the rearranged body parts. "Is this really Doc?"

Laura replied, "Yes, or should I say, what's left of Doctor Fletcher. The last photo in the group is the remains of Casey Ross."

"We used to call him Cowboy. Everyone had nicknames. In this picture, he looks like raw meat. What happened?"

"Someone bull-whipped him to death."

Sinclair could see Dunbar was ready to jump out of his seat to ask the next question. He motioned for Josh to remain seated and then asked the Jew, "Doesn't it kind of make you wonder what kind of death the killer has in mind for you?"

Jerome's blood went cold and the officers could see the thought flash through his mind. He tried to show calm as he answered, "Why would anyone want to kill me?"

Sinclair's patience with Josh, was really wearing thin. He had to keep one eye on the inspector, while trying to question the Jew. He wanted to ask the obvious question as much as Dunbar, but he was following their carefully planned script, when the FBI agent asked, "The way I look at it, you are either the killer or a potential victim. Which is it and why?"

"I am not the killer!" Jerome was hesitant to consider his situation. Pensively, he asked, "Besides, why would I be a potential victim? After all, what could the killer possibly want from me?"

Josh could contain himself no longer. He jumped to his feet, pointed a finger at Jerome, and asked Sinclair, "Why in the hell don't you ask him about the damned tontine?"

Everyone in the room turned to hear Josh's tirade, so they missed the shocked look on the Jew's face. Jerome had time to recover before attentions turned back to him. "Tontine? What is a tontine?"

The set-up Sinclair had been carefully working toward had been derailed by Dunbar. He realized any further pursuit would only get a denial from their suspect. He decided to let the question pass unanswered. It was sufficient that Miller knew, they knew about the pact. Sinclair decided to let Jerome think about it. The FBI agent changed the subject. "I think we've taken up quite enough of your time, Mr. Miller."

"What?" screamed Josh, who was quickly silenced by a raised hand from Sinclair.

"As I was saying, Mr. Miller. We're going to interview the remaining names on your list. If it isn't too much to ask, would you be so kind as to tell me something about each of them?"

Confused by the change of demeanor, Jerome replied, "Let's see. There's William Johnson in Iowa. We used to call him Red because of the color of his hair. I can't believe he's a murderer."

Laura asked, "What about the one in Chicago?"

"Bambridge? We called him Professor. He used to carry and smoke a damned pipe in combat. Always acted smarter than the rest of us. No, I can't see him doing it. All he cares about is his work. He actually became a professor at Northwestern University in the Physics Department. Damned fool always sends me articles for the newsletter. He thinks they're interesting, but I can't understand a word he says."

Sinclair wanted to know, "What about the others, here in New York City?"

"Brownie runs a diner in Harlem."

"Isn't that Leroy Williams, the black man?"

"Yeah, he's black and I know what you're thinking. Sure we were upset when they sent a colored guy to be in our outfit, but we loved him. We didn't call him Brownie because of his skin. He carried a Browning Automatic Rifle. Now, he's a possibility."

"Why would Mr. Williams be a likely suspect?"

"Recently he's been asking to borrow money from the group. I guess business is a little slow for him. Maybe he did it for the money."

Sinclair jumped on the Jew's slip up by asking, "Why would killing these guys get him any closer to money?"

Jerome recovered with, "Did I imply that? What I meant to say is, he might have asked these guys for money and killed them to avoid paying them back or something."

Again Sinclair knew denials waited for any further questions, so he asked, "What about this Carletti fellow?"

"Fingers! Now there's a piece of work. Claims and acts like he's some big shot in the Mafia or something. Who knows. Maybe he would. Maybe there's some vendetta working here. He was always threatening to have us killed. We all thought it was a big joke."

Agent Sinclair stood up and said, "You've been very helpful, Mr. Miller. We'll take up no more of your time. Thank you."

Josh bolted up from his chair and started saying, "What are you... Why don't you... He didn't..."

Special Agent Sinclair held out his hand in a stop gesture and then motioned for the team to leave. Laura stood and started pushing a still grumbling inspector toward the door. She whispered in his ear, "There must be a good reason. Shut up. He'll tell us outside."

When the group got across the street and a few doors down the block, Sinclair turned on Dunbar, poking a finger into the inspector's chest, saying, "The next time we agree to a plan of interrogation, I expect you to stick to it. If you don't, you'll find yourself on the outside. Do you understand me?"

"Cut the crap. The son of a bitch knows what is going on."

"No kidding. What gave it away to you? "

Laura said, "It's also obvious he isn't ready to tell us."

"Good conclusion, detective. This guy is going nowhere. If he's not the killer, he's got to be sweating things. Let's let him sweat. In the mean time, let's get out to the other two here and find out what they know."

Josh sarcastically said, "You didn't get all the answers you needed out of this guy."

The FBI agent was still upset with Dunbar. He stared directly into Josh's eyes, but spoke as if he were somewhere else. "I'd rather be rid of the inspector for awhile. Detective Miles and I will take a cab over to Harlem and talk to this Williams character. You two take the car and drive over to Mr. Carletti's. When you're done, come pick us up at the restaurant. Got it?"

Dunbar looked at Laura as if she was supposed to defend him. Instead, she turned away from him and started looking for a taxi to hail. Dunbar grabbed the local FBI agent by the shoulder and said, "Let's go, bud. The air is a little too cold for me here."

In the cab, neither Miles nor Sinclair spoke for a bit. Finally, the FBI agent asked, "Was there something going on back there, between the two of you, I should know about?"

"Like what?"

"Oh, I don't know. It just seemed like he was looking at you for help?"

"It's probably nothing. You chewed him out in front of a woman. He probably was trying to save face."

"He deserved to be chewed out for it."

Laura decided to defend Josh by offering, "He was just doing what he thought was best to help out."

The agent thought for a moment and looked down to see a good portion of Laura's legs showing out from the partially parted coat. "This may sound funny, but I keep forgetting you are a woman."

"What?"

"I mean, you're so much like a regular cop."

"And what is that supposed to mean? I am a regular detective. I hold my own. I'm a damned good cop."

"I didn't mean anything by it. Look, I said the wrong thing. Hey, I remember how good you were the last time we worked together."

Laura was still a bit miffed, but it felt good that she put him back on his heels for second. "I didn't think you remembered. I didn't seem too high on your priority list at the time."

"Yes, I suppose it might have felt that way. That was business then."

Laura was curious when she asked him, "Isn't this business now?"

Realizing he was walking pretty close to the edge, Lewis measured his words carefully. "This is serious business, and I'll try not to put my other foot in my mouth like I did a few seconds ago. I admire your professionalism and respect you as a police officer. At the same time, my year in Paris has given me a deeper appreciation for the fairer sex. In this cab, sitting alone with you, it is hard not to notice you are a very beautiful woman."

Laura wanted the respect, but also didn't mind the attention. After all, the FBI man was refined, educated, well traveled, and certainly on the fast track in law enforcement.

Laura still did not completely trust him, but for the sake of getting information and keeping her personal options open, there was no use in slamming the door shut. She shifted in her seat slightly, raising her knees a bit causing the coat to slide back on her legs a few inches. She told him, "I think we're almost at our destination. Some other time, you'll have to tell me about your time in Paris."

Sinclair paid the driver and they got out of the cab. The two looked slightly out of place in the middle of Harlem. They noticed the sign on the building. It read, "Yo Mama's Home Cooking."

The diner went eerily quiet when the two walked inside. A woman behind the counter asked, "What can we do for you officers?"

"How did you know we were police?" asked Laura.

"Ain't never no white people come in here saves the police or the health department. Pay no mind to it. Ain't no big thang. Now what y'all want?"

Sinclair said, “We're looking for Leroy Williams. Is he around?”

The woman turned around and screamed through a small window in the wall, “Leroy! The man need to talk to you.”

A few seconds later, a large black man came out of the kitchen. He was wearing a heavily soiled apron with no shirt underneath and he was holding a big spatula like a weapon. The most noticeable feature was the big afro haircut on his head. “If you're from the health department, I've got a hair net in back.”

Sinclair whipped out his badge and said, “No, Mr. Williams, I'm Special Agent Lewis Sinclair with the FBI and this is Detective Laura Miles of the Los Angeles police department. We'd like to ask you a few questions.”

“What you doing all the way out here from L. A.?”

Laura answered, “I think that's one of the things Agent Sinclair would like to explain. Is there somewhere private where we can talk?”

“Look around. What you see is what I've got. Ain't no one here gonna pay no attention. Let's just sit over in that corner booth. Just a second.” Leroy hollered over for some woman to go back into the kitchen and take over his cooking duties.

The group sat down and Leroy offered them coffee. After it arrived, Sinclair began with, “Mr. Williams, are you familiar with the newsletter, 'Here's To Your Health'?”

“Sure I am. Some of my buddies from the war and I stay in touch with it. Why?”

“Did you know that five of them are dead?”

“Say what? What are you saying?”

“According to Jerome Miller, the one's you called Tinker, Sarge, Doc, Cowboy, and Moocher are dead.”

Leroy was shocked and took a drink of his coffee. His hands were shaking as he raised the cup to his lips. "Damn! How'd they die? Car accident or something?"

"I regret to inform you, they were murdered."

"Killed?" Leroy let the information settle in before asking, "What did the Jew boy have to say about it?"

"That doesn't matter, Mr. Williams. We're here to find out what you know. Do you have any idea why someone would be killing your friends?"

Leroy took another drink of coffee and then wanted to know, "How did you folks find me anyway?"

Laura jumped in saying, "We actually got the names from Mr. Miller, but it was the tattoo which linked the group together. Have you got one of those tattoos?"

"Yeah. A lot of good it does on my black ass. That was a white boy's group all the way. I'm sure they'd just have soon cut me out of my fair share."

"Your share of what?" asked Sinclair.

Realizing he had slipped, Leroy changed the subject a bit. "Do you have any idea who's been doing the killing?"

Detective Miles offered, "Mr. Miller suggested you might know or in some way be involved."

"That damned Jew! Money got tight around here once and I asked if he'd print a request for help in the newsletter. Never ask a Jew for money. I bet he thinks I'm knocking off these guys to get rich."

Sinclair returned to his previous question. "Why would killing these five make you rich?"

Leroy realized he'd better shut up before he gave the whole thing away. He smiled at the officers and said, "Look. I never leave this place. I live upstairs. This place has been in my family for forty years. Let me set you straight. What you white people do to each other is your own business. I didn't do it and I ain't telling you nothin' more."

As Brownie was finishing his statement, Dunbar came walking in the door. He stood at Sinclair's shoulder. The FBI agent pulled out a business card and handed it to Leroy. "If you think of anything else, please call me at the number written on the card. They can get hold of me wherever I am."

Leroy looked at the card and then asked, "And who's this cracker?"

"This is Inspector Dunbar of the San Francisco police. He's here helping us with the investigation. Would you mind if we sat here for a few minutes to discuss things?"

"Ain't no thing. I've got the best coffee in town. You folks get hungry, well, it's on the house. Now I've got to get back in the kitchen."

Dunbar took Brownie's place at the booth. He thanked the waitress for the coffee and asked if she'd take a cup out to the local FBI agent who remained in the car outside. Josh took a sip of the coffee and then asked, "Did you guy's have any luck with this guy?"

Laura answered, as Sinclair still seemed miffed with Josh. "No. This guy's as tight-lipped as the other. They're hiding something."

Josh looked the FBI agent in the eye as he asked, "Did you find out what he knew of the tontine?"

Sinclair answered sarcastically, "No, we didn't ask him about the tontine. " Behind a strategically placed hand, Josh gestured obscenely at the agent, with the middle finger of the other hand. After a few seconds, Sinclair relented and asked, "So, what did you find out from Carletti?"

"You wouldn't believe this guy. I thought I was in some old gangster movie. This Carletti character has his office at some concrete plant. You know, the kind where they make up a batch and deliver it in those cement-mixer trucks. He's got what looks like a construction trailer on the outside. It's a really big one. Once you get inside, you'd think you were in a mansion. This place is a palace."

"Enough of the Better Homes and Gardens tour," declared Lewis. "What did he have to tell us?"

"That's what was so great about this. Here we are in this construction area and outside his trailer are these two thugs in fancy suits. They call into the trailer on a telephone and the next thing you know, some other suit comes out to tell us Mr. Carletti will see us now."

"Would you get to the point?" asked a frustrated FBI agent.

"So we go into this room, his office, and it's huge. There's walnut paneling everywhere. Carletti is sitting behind his big desk and some girl is giving him a manicure while we talk. If this guy ain't connected to the Mafia, he's sure putting on a good show."

Sinclair was getting impatient. "What did he know?"

"I asked him what he knew about his war buddies. He already knew they were dead."

"What did he say?"

"He told me it was regrettable news to hear of the early demise of his former associates."

"How did he know?" asked Laura.

"When I asked him if Mr. Miller had called, Carletti said, "I don't ask nothing from that Jew." When I asked him again how he knew, he just told me he had his sources."

Sinclair wrinkled his nose and lips, then mockingly said, "I suppose you asked him about the tontine."

"You're damned right I did."

"And he told you he knew nothing about it," said Sinclair firmly.

A bit crestfallen, Josh said, "Right. He denied knowing anything about the murders, claimed he'd never been out of town, and then suggested I should leave."

Laura wanted to know, "Did he seem the least bit worried he might be the next victim?"

"Yeah. I asked him about it and he gestured around the room and said it should be obvious he had nothing to fear." Josh looked for the waitress and signaled for more coffee. "You know that Williams guy was right. This is some of the best coffee I've ever had."

Chapter 27

The private jet belonging to the FBI was on final approach into Des Moines, Iowa. Three passengers were on board. They were rushing to the latest scene of a murdered, tattooed veteran. Approaching from the southeast, the plane passed over endless farms and acres of corn, soybeans, and alfalfa. The city of Des Moines remained out of sight to the north.

Sinclair looked at the rural scenery passing by his window and asked, "They do have an airport, don't they?"

Laura offered, "It was a lucky thing we were only in Chicago when the news came in. It was amazing how fast your FBI people were. We got the news less than three hours ago and now we're nearly in Des Moines."

The jet landed and rolled to a stop at one of the hangars where a car waited for the passengers. A local FBI agent stood near the car and an Iowa State Police cruiser waited to give the group an escort to the scene of the crime.

One by one they climbed out of the jet and into the waiting car. Once loaded, the entourage started their trip into the country behind the flash of red lights and the wail of a plaintive siren.

Sinclair asked the local agent, "How did the murder take place?"

The man said, "At first, they thought it was a farm accident. Once they dug into it a bit more, they realized it was a murder."

Laura offered, "Well at least we can write off the professor in Chicago as a suspect. After all, we were with him when news of the murder came in. He couldn't have done it."

"That certainly makes our life a bit easier," said Dunbar. "Now we can concentrate all our efforts in New York."

"I don't agree with your simplistic view," said Sinclair.

Josh, a bit perturbed at the negative response, asked, "Why are you always on my case?"

"Somebody has to."

Josh pointed his finger at the agent. "Some day you're going to fall off of the high horse you're riding. When you do, I hope you break your neck."

The FBI agent was still irritated, but he at least respected the way Josh fought back. "What you said is true. I'm saying we shouldn't concentrate our efforts in New York."

"Why the hell not?" spewed Dunbar. "The professor couldn't have done it. We were with him, so that leaves us the three in New York as suspects."

"I'm not talking about suspects. I'm talking about stopping this thing right now. I'm saying we stop it, in Chicago, before the next one is killed."

Laura inquired, "What are you saying? Chicago? How do we stop it?"

"The way I figure it," said Sinclair, "this guy is heading East. The first two murders were in San Francisco. The next two were in Los Angeles. Then, we had the one in Oklahoma and now Des Moines. I'm betting the next victim will be the guy in Chicago."

Laura and Josh let the thought sink in a bit before Josh acquiesced and said, "I didn't think about it until you said something."

The agent couldn't resist the opening. "That's just my point. You don't think before opening your mouth."

"Fuck you, Sinclair."

Laura tried to bring some calm to the situation by asking the FBI agent, "Why do you think the killer is doing it this way?"

Sinclair replied, "My guess is he's just being systematic about it."

Puzzled, Laura wanted to know, "What makes you say that?"

"Everything this killer did, has been methodical. Whoever is doing it, is not in a hurry. No, this man's a stickler for detail and he's very patient. It's almost as if the killer is taking pride in his work."

"So, you still think this is the work of one individual and not some hired hands?" wondered Josh.

"Definitely. I told you this is personal, very personal. Whoever this is takes the time to get in close to the victim, without suspicion, so they must be known to the victim. No, I'd bet my career it's one of the tontine members."

The cars rolled into the driveway of a farm, a few miles south of the airport. They rolled past the barns and out into the cornfields. The tall corn blocked most of their field of vision, so they really couldn't tell how far out into the field they had driven when suddenly they popped out into a cleared section. The road paralleled a large expanse of cornstalk stubble. At one end was a corn harvester, its nose buried in the corn rows. A grain trailer was in tow behind it, a small mountain of corn sticking out above the rim of the trailer.

The car stopped and the group of officers got out of the car and walked toward the machinery. A dozen local law enforcement personnel were pouring over the equipment, taking pictures and looking for other clues. As the newly arrived group neared the scene, another local FBI agent came over and pulled Sinclair aside for a brief discussion. In a minute or two, they separated and the local man shouted for everyone but the coroner to get away from the equipment. When they had cleared, Sinclair took Laura and Josh over to make their own examination.

"You must be Dr. Parker," Sinclair said with authority. "I'm Special Agent Sinclair. This is Detective Miles from Los Angeles and this is Inspector Dunbar from San Francisco."

The coroner was wearing rubber gloves. He gestured to them as an excuse to not shake their hands. "Glad to meet you all."

Sinclair asked, "How did the victim die?"

"The victim got caught in the corn picker. Hell of a way for a man to die if you ask me."

"Why is it?" wondered Laura.

"Come with me," signaled the coroner. When they got to the front of the huge device, he explained, "A corn picker has these big finger-like things which travel an inch or two above the ground. These big blades chop the cornstalk off at the ground and pulls it farther up into the strippers. You can't see them here, but they strip the ears of corn from the stalk and feed them into the shuckers. The leaves and the stalks are chewed up and spit out the side into the field."

"What happens to the ears of corn?" asked Josh.

Moving to the side of the machine, the coroner pointed to the fifteen foot tall sides of the hardware. "Inside there are a number of tumblers and things which rip the kernels of corn from the corncob. The cobs are shredded and spit into the field while the corn kernels are pumped up through that tube and thrown into the trailer."

Having never been near this kind of thing, Josh had no idea his next question was so stupid. "Don't all those blades and screens turn the corn to soup?"

The coroner realized Josh was naive and tried to explain, "The corn is left standing out in the fields to dry. It isn't harvested until the kernels are hard. The abrasion of the rollers and blades knocks the dried kernels from the cob. Here, let me show you." Dr. Parker reached out and took an ear from a nearby stalk, pulled the dried husks from the ear, and with his hand rolled off a few kernels. "See they just fall off the cob with a little pulling."

Sinclair wanted to know, "You said this was a particularly bad way for a person to die. Why is that?"

"The poor sucker sees it coming and has time to suffer. Those blades up front most likely chops their feet off at the ankle, then, leg first, they are pulled up into the strippers. The flesh is pulled off the bones of the legs. I've even seen one man where the torso got hung up in the V-notch at the top of the fingers. The strippers just ripped the poor devil in half at the waist and left him hanging on up there."

The group agreed with the coroner's opinion of the death. Sinclair asked, "So how did the driver get in front of those cutters."

"It couldn't have been the driver," said the coroner matter of factly.

"What do you mean?"

"In the old days maybe, but not on a newer model like this one. These have a dead man's switch in them."

Josh asked, "What's that?"

"There's an interlock in the cab. Someone has to be in the cab holding it down. If you don't, everything stops. Most of these accidents occur when something jams up the strippers. The driver stays in the cab while someone reaches in with a tool or something to un-jam them."

Josh thought for a moment and then inquired, "What's left of a body after it goes through this thing?"

"Not much," said the coroner. "If you want to climb up here, I'll show you."

They climbed the ladders welded to the sides of the grain trailer and looked at the small mountain of golden kernels. Sticking out near the summit was the partial remnants of a hand reaching a couple fingers to the sky. A few shards of bone were visible along with bits of cloth and leather. One item caught Josh's eye. A human ear lay on top of the corn in the exact position it would have on a head. He couldn't resist the chance to joke, "Now I know what they mean by an ear of corn."

The group came down from the trailer. Sinclair asked the coroner, "I've got two questions for you. What told you this wasn't an accident and how did you know to call us?"

"Well the accident part of it was easy. It was the calling you folks which was interesting."

"Why was it, Doctor?"

Dr. Parker pointed up and told the group, "Take a look in the cab."

They climbed up the machine and opened the door. At first they didn't notice anything, but then on the steering wheel, they found it. There was a small patch of human skin, tied at the corners and pulled tight with some baling string. The skin had the tattoo from Paris and tucked under the edge of the skin was a business card for "William 'Red' Johnson, Farm Insurance Salesman".

The group crawled down from the cab. Laura was feeling a bit sickened and Josh tried to comfort her. Sinclair kept a stiff upper lip as he talked to the coroner. "I thought this was the victim's equipment."

"Nope. Wasn't even his farm. The victim's car is a few rows over in the corn. His briefcase is still on the seat. Damnedest thing I've ever seen. What about you?"

Sinclair looked back toward the cab of the corn picker and then said, "Not quite, but it's rapidly getting there. Okay, I've got what I need for now. Your people can finish their work and forward the report to the FBI office in Chicago. They'll get it to me there."

Sinclair's group returned to the car and started back to the Des Moines airport. Once they were back on paved roads, Sinclair told the local FBI agent, "When you get back to the office, call the Chicago and New York police. I want tight surveillance on the four remaining members of this club. I want to know where they are and what they're doing every minute of the day."

Before boarding the jet to return to Chicago, Sinclair found an empty office with a telephone and dialed the number of the Jew. The phone rang and connected. "Mr. Miller. This is Special Agent Sinclair."

"I've already said everything I'm going to tell you."

"That may be true, but I just wanted to let you know I'm in Iowa."

"Red?"

"Yes. Your club has one less member."

"How did he die?"

"I don't see why it matters to you, but he was shredded into a hundred tiny bits in a piece of farm machinery."

"Sounds like an accident to me."

"No. It was murder all right. It was a particularly nasty murder. You can continue to live a fantasy if you want, but there's only four of you left. Are you sure there isn't something you want to tell me?"

"Why would I change my mind?"

"Because if you haven't noticed, these murders are heading east. Whoever it is, they're heading your way." Sinclair slammed the phone receiver down, leaving the Jew listening to a dial tone.

Chapter 28

The crystal chandeliers, gleaming silver, and twinkling candle-light were everything one would expect at a swank Michigan Avenue hotel in Chicago. Special Agent Sinclair sampled the wine offered to him by the wine steward. He signaled his satisfaction and accepted the wine. The steward poured two glasses, his and another for his dining partner, Laura Miles.

He lifted his glass as a toast and offered, "One of the fringe benefits of working for J. Edgar Hoover. Only the best will do."

Laura tapped his glass with hers, sampled the wine and then said, "You can say that again. In Los Angeles, we're lucky to get hot dogs and stay at the Flea Bag Inn. Still, isn't this hotel and restaurant pushing it a bit?"

"Everything is relative. It depends more on how you justify the expenditure and less on how much it costs."

"Are you telling me you lie to your boss?"

The FBI agent swirled the wine in his glass as he nonchalantly said, "No. I don't have to lie. I have more freedom as a Special Agent. My reputation and stature in the department allows me more freedom."

"Well, however you justify it, I could get used to doing all my police work this way, but I do have one question."

"Ask away."

"Why am I here and Inspector Dunbar is not?"

"Don't you like my company?"

Laura measured her answer, not wanting to explain what there was of a relationship with Josh for fear of slamming shut the door of opportunity with this man. "I enjoy the company. I just wondered why you did not invite him."

"I suppose this isn't an easy question to answer, so give me a chance to explain. First, I've had lunches and dinners with each of you, alone, at different times. I never paid any attention to it."

"That may be true, but you can hardly equate hamburgers with filet mignon."

Sinclair chuckled a bit, "Yes. I suppose you can't. On the other hand, you have helped to make my point. Why would I waste a dinner like this on him, when I can share this evening with a beautiful woman such as yourself?"

Laura wasn't seeking a compliment, just an explanation. His statement caught her by surprise, causing her to blush slightly. She needed to get her composure back. She took a sip of wine and then said, "Whatever the reason, it feels good to dress up a bit and eat from real plates for a change."

"You look magnificent." Noticing a strange look on Laura's face, he paused for a second and then apologized. "Forgive me for being forward, again it must be the time I spent in Paris."

Laura had her chance to deflect the conversation away from herself. "Earlier, you mentioned your reputation with the FBI. How did you get stationed in France?"

"I have a perfect record. I've never had an unsolved case and I've never failed to catch the criminal."

"You've never made a mistake?"

"In the FBI, you can't make mistakes. You do and you're working some back office in Altoona shuffling papers. On the other hand, if you keep your nose clean and do great work, you move up quickly. One day, an official from our French equivalent, the Surete, was visiting our office. I minored in French during college, so I walked up to him and struck up a conversation."

"Is that what impressed your superiors and got you assigned to Paris?"

"Not really. The official asked me to escort him for the rest of his visit and serve as his translator. A few years later, there was an exchange program between the two countries. The bureau needed someone to go to France and show them some of our FBI techniques. The same French official asked for me personally."

Laura finished the wine in her glass and Sinclair wasted no time in refilling it. The bottle was empty and he signaled to the wine steward to bring another. Laura asked, "What was it like to live in Paris?"

"Do you like the wine?"

"Yes. It's very good."

"Well, that's sort of what it's like to live in Paris. It is one thing to learn about wines, but quite another to live the experience. You can drive into the country, stop by some small farm, and walk the vine rows with the farmer. Next thing you know, his wife brings out a basket of breads and bottles of wine, and you're sitting in the vineyard taking in the sun."

"Is it true they all drink wine, even the children?"

"Absolutely. The children drink wine which has been diluted with water. The adults drink wine with every meal, much like we drink water. Oh, and the food is wonderful. Even street-side cafes have food rivaling some of America's finest restaurants. Paris truly is a sensuous city."

Laura took another long sip of her wine and then asked him, "Why do you keep talking about Paris in a sexual way?"

"Not sexual, sensual. The city excites all of your senses. The sights of the lights around Paris. The smell of flowers in the air. The sound of music filling the air from around every street corner. You can't imagine it. You must experience it."

Laura emptied her glass of wine and Lewis quickly refilled it. She could feel the wine starting to go to her head, but she found herself fascinated by Sinclair's tales of Paris. The warmth of the wine-glow relaxed her to a point where his tales of fancy swept her away in her imagination. She also found herself becoming aroused by his stories. This man was such a contrast to Josh.

Josh was simple, safe, and familiar. Sinclair was traveled, exotic, and unknown. She listened to his stories of France and become wrapped in the romantic life it portrayed. It was late and the waiter was clearing the last of the dinner plates when Sinclair asked, "We've got to go now, but if you'd like we could continue this discussion in my suite."

"You wouldn't be trying to take advantage of a starry-eyed girl, would you?"

"I take offense at your accusation. After everything I've told you about Paris, I thought you'd have realized I am a gentleman. I ask you to my suite as a gentleman to continue a lovely evening of conversation in the presence of a lovely lady."

As they walked down the hall, he lifted her hand into the bend of his elbow in an elegant gesture of civility. She felt herself drawn to him. No doubt part of it was the wine and rich food, but part of it was her. She wanted him.

He unlocked the door, walked her into the room, and turned on the light. Laura commented, "Wow. I only have a regular room. This place is fantastic. Look at the furniture."

"Do you like it?"

"Absolutely." Laura dropped her purse on the settee and kicked off her high heels, which lowered her to the same height as the agent. She sidled up to him slowly and stopped inches from him. She asked, "Would you do me a favor?"

"What would it be?"

"Speak French to me, even if I can't understand it."

" Toi et moi allons comprende la langue de l'amour."

Simultaneously they pulled each other together in a passionate, full body embrace. Frantically their hands ran up and down each other's bodies. The warmth of the wine in Laura's body was replaced with the fire of the passion building inside. Their kiss was long, deep, and slow.

Desperate for air, they separated and Sinclair said, " Embrasse moie encore idiot."

Laura pulled Sinclair's coat back and over his shoulders, throwing it to the floor. Bit by bit, he pulled up the hem of her skirt until he could clamp his hand over her silk panties and squeeze her firm buttocks. He pulled her to him and she did not resist.

Between feverish kisses, they continued to remove clothing. Laura slid his shoulder holster and gun off his arms and threw them onto his coat. The FBI agent fumbled with the buttons on the jacket of her suit. Finally, with her assistance he was able to remove her coat and look at the pink lace bra holding up her ample breasts. "Mon dieu! Je crois que je suis au paradi," he gasped.

She pulled the straps of his suspenders down and let them hang from his waist, while she ripped open the front of his shirt and slammed her chest against his. The momentum caused them to fall backward. Fortunately a wall was a few feet behind them to stop their fall.

Laura began to pull at the tails of his shirt, pulling them out of his pants. Sinclair buried his head in her cleavage and felt the beads of sweat collecting in the valley. He slid her skirt up around her waist and plunged his hand under the back of her panties to pull her tighter.

"Take me here. Take me now."

He spun her around so she was pinned against the wall and said, " Tes souhaits sont mes commandes."

A knock sounded at the door.

The two panting lovers paused for a moment. Sinclair put his hand gently over Laura's lips as she whispered, "Who could that be?"

The knocking started again, but quickly changed to pounding.

Sinclair backed away from Laura. She picked up her clothing and he went to get his gun from the discarded shoulder holster. Sinclair waited near the door. From the other side he heard, "Hey, Sinclair. It's Dunbar. I know you're in there. The lights are on and I heard you speaking that French gibberish."

Laura sobered up immediately. The warmth she felt moments ago was replaced by beads of cold sweat. She searched for the rest of her clothes and started to dress as quickly as she could. Sinclair relaxed the grip on his gun and spoke through the door, "You sound like you've been drinking."

"Yeah, I've been drinking, but I'm not drunk. Now are you going to let me in or not?"

Sinclair looked down at his disheveled clothes and said, "It's late and I just got out of the shower. Can't this wait until the morning?"

"I was just dropping off the damned report you asked me to get on Sergeant Cummings' service record. I'll just slide it under the door. See you in the morning."

Sinclair heard Josh walk off down the hall and then turned back to Laura. He was surprised to see her fully dressed. He put his gun down on the end table and said, "Quest ce quice passe?"

"I'm sorry, but I think the moment has come and gone. Now that I've had time to think, I don't know if this was a really good idea anyway."

Frustrated and emotionally wounded, he realized she was right. Pushing her now would not be worth the effort and might destroy any future chances he might have with her. A strategic retreat now might keep his possibilities open another time. Collecting his wits, he took her hand and blew a kiss across her knuckles and said, "Merci beau coup. Maybe some other time."

The telephone rang before Laura could reply. Sinclair walked over and picked up the receiver. "Hello. Yes, this is he. What? How could it have happened? No. Don't touch a thing. We'll be there as soon as we can."

"What's happened?" asked Laura.

"Despite the finest efforts of the Chicago police department, someone got to Professor Bambridge. He's dead. Go fix yourself up in the bathroom. We've got to get down there."

Chapter 29

As the trio rounded the corner in the basement of the Physics Research Building, they ran into a small crowd of Chicago policemen, drinking coffee and talking about the murder. Sinclair demanded, "Who the hell is in charge here?"

A couple of the officers pointed to a smaller group of plain-clothes police officers standing outside the door of one of the laboratories. One of the men turned around and said, "I'm Lieutenant Spencer. Are you from the FBI?"

"I'm Special Agent Sinclair. These two are Detective Miles and Inspector Dunbar. They're with me. Now, how in the hell did this happen?"

Without showing any undue concern, the officer said, "Someone came in and whacked the professor in there."

Sinclair could not believe the stupidity he was hearing. "I know that, you moron. Your people were supposed to prevent this from happening. What I want to know is, how did it happened right under your noses?"

"Hold on there a second. No one told us to watch this guy every second and they didn't tell us anything about protecting this guy. We were just told to keep tabs on his whereabouts. We knew where he was."

The FBI agent just shook his head. "We told you to keep a tight surveillance on a possible murder target."

"We did. We kept men outside the building, his office, and outside his house. Wherever he went, we went. What's your problem?"

Sinclair started poking his finger into the palm of his other hand, saying, "Let me see if I can use small enough words for you to understand. We knew someone was going to try and kill this guy. You were told to make sure nothing happened to him. What part of that didn't you understand?"

The group of Chicago officers was not happy with the agent's attitude and drew in tight behind their boss in a show of solidarity. With this support, the lieutenant defended his men. "We did what we were supposed to do. We followed this guy and kept close tabs on him. He taught two classes today, worked in his office until six, grabbed a chicken salad sandwich in the cafeteria, and showed up here at seven. No one gets into this building without security clearance. We kept one car on the street and one officer at the top of the stairs over there. What more were we supposed to do?"

In a mocking and accusatory tone, Sinclair fumed, "I knew we shouldn't have left this up to you local boys. I wanted to use FBI agents, but no, we had to show consideration to the local law enforcement agencies. Well, you screwed up!"

"Watch it G-man! We did all we could."

"So how'd he end up dead?"

The groups stood staring at each other, waiting to see which would move first. The testosterone stand-off continued until another man came out of the lab and said, "If you gorillas are through flexing your muscles, I'm willing to tell you what happened in here."

For a few more seconds, the FBI agent and the Chicago officer remained staring at each other. It was Laura and Josh who turned around to break the stalemate. Laura extended her hand to the man and said, "I'm Detective Miles and this is Inspector Dunbar. Who are you?"

"I'm the medical examiner. Everyone calls me Buddy."

The FBI agent turned around in a huff and squeezed between Josh and Laura to take over control of the investigation. He made it clear it was his show and not theirs by his attitude. "Okay, Buddy. Let's go see what we've got here. Keep those other baboons out of here."

The group walked into the brightly, but eerily lit lab. It was not what they expected. The room was huge and tall. The colors were mostly white and stainless steel. Large steel tanks lined one wall and were almost two stories tall. There were a few large, open stainless steel vats. Beams and tracks stretched across the ceiling. Movable hoists with chains were suspended from the tracks.

The only real color in the room came from the hundreds of large wires and cables, running to and from various kinds of electrical panels and testing equipment. The coroner stopped the small group a couple of feet into the room and gestured for the group to look around as if there was something important for them to see.

Josh wanted to know, "So where's the body?"

"You're looking at it."

"What?"

"Look around. The body is all around you."

Sinclair was not amused. "Look, Buddy, I'm not in any mood for games. Where is the body?"

The group started peering over, around, and under the hardware, looking for the body. Suddenly Laura screamed a brief shriek. "What's the matter?" asked Josh.

Laura held her hand over her mouth in shock and pointed at the floor. The two men knelt down and looked at a small item on the floor. It lay in one of the shadows cast by the stark white lights. As their eyes adjusted to the light, they realized they were looking at part of a man's finger. The men looked at each other and simultaneously said, "What the hell?"

As they looked around, they realized there were tiny bits of body parts all around the lab floor. The little blobs of flesh were not large, but here and there were parts large enough to identify a toe, a nose, a bit of tongue. The coroner spoke from behind the group, "Fascinating, isn't it?"

Laura had gotten a grip on herself enough to ask the coroner, "Was there an explosion? Did this guy get blown up?"

Josh answered her question first with, “Couldn't have been. There's no smoke, no burn marks on the floor or walls. Besides, an explosion would have set off alarms and alerted the policemen.”

“Right you are,” said the coroner. “We're dealing with cryogenics here.”

Now it was Sinclair who wanted to know, “What are you saying?”

“Your victim has been shattered.” Noticing the skeptical faces, Buddy continued, “I thought you'd have trouble with this, so let me demonstrate.”

The coroner opened a small, stainless steel canister. Fog flowed out of it. The coroner picked up an apple and dropped it into the canister. After a few seconds, he used long tongs to pick the apple out of the can. He held it out at arm's length and then dropped it to the floor. The apple shattered into a thousand pieces.

“How'd you do that?” asked Laura.

The coroner explained, “This canister is filled with liquid nitrogen. It's temperature is several hundred degrees below zero. You drop something into it and it's almost instantly frozen solid. Drop the item to a hard surface and it shatters like glass.”

“So you're telling me this guy was frozen and then dropped?” wondered Sinclair.

“Yup. That's what happened. Those big tanks back there are filled with liquid nitrogen and they have pipes which lead into these insulated vats. My guess is the professor was put into one of these until he was frozen solid and then lifted to the ceiling with one of those hoists. If you look at the body chips, they spread out from one point back behind the vat over there. I figure whoever it was, dropped the body and the fragments slid across the room to where you find them. ”

The three officers let the profound impact of their physics lesson sink in. They looked at each other and collectively felt the chills flow over their bodies. Sinclair was about to say something when the coroner said, "You might say this guy really went to pieces." This caused an uneasy chuckle to break out.

Josh wondered, "Have you been able to check all of the body pieces?"

"Are you kidding? Pieces bounced onto tables, into the corners, and onto bookshelves. Hell, I found a patch of scalp in somebody's coffee cup. Why did you ask?"

"Specifically, I'm wondering if there's a patch of skin with a tattoo on it laying around."

"I suppose nothing stops us from looking for it. If you three want to help me, we'll see if we can find it."

The group put on rubber gloves. Using pencils, screwdrivers, and tweezers, they picked through small blobs of skin, bone, and internal organs. After about twenty minutes, Laura called from behind a coat rack. "I've got a piece over here."

The three men joined her and looked down at the now thawed portion of skin. The color of ink matched the other tattoos, but this had only a portion of the border and the word "Paris" on it. A few feet away, Josh spotted another piece with more of the tattoo. On top of a box, the coroner found some more. Buddy asked, "Was that what you were looking for?"

"In a way," said Sinclair. "Well. I think we've got what we need for the moment." Reaching out his hand toward the coroner and then realizing they both had on gloves, the agent retracted his hand and said, "Thanks for your help, Buddy. We'll let your people finish. Send the report to the local FBI office and let it catch up with me. We've got to head for New York."

The three officers walked out of the lab. Sinclair could not resist sending one last dirty look toward the Chicago officers. The trio marched down the hall and outside the building. Once outside, in the breaking dawn, Josh wanted to know, "Why the bum's rush? Why did you suddenly hustle us out of there?"

Sinclair explained, "Because there's been a big change in this case."

Laura asked, "What makes you think so?"

"On this murder, the killer didn't care if we found the tattoo. That means the killer knows we've figured out who the potential victims are."

"Does this change the way we handle things?" wondered Dunbar.

"It might. Look. Here's what we're going to do when we get back to the hotel. Laura, I want you to go over all our notes. I want to know if we'd spoken to all of the remaining suspects before the death in Iowa."

Josh reacted to the FBI agent calling Laura by her first name. Until now it had always been Detective Miles. He wondered about the change. His musing was broken by Sinclair saying, "Dunbar, I want you to call New York and check out all three suspects' alibis. I want to know where they've been the last forty-eight hours."

Dunbar replied, "I can do it, but has any of us had any sleep?"

Laura and Lewis looked at each other and then looked away. Josh noticed and shrugged his shoulders inquisitively at her. Laura wrinkled her nose at him as if it was none of his business and then ignored him.

Sinclair looked at his watch, "Yeah. I suppose we could all use a nap. Okay. We'll go back to the hotel and grab some sleep, but I want you both to get me the information I asked for and meet me for a late lunch, say, the coffee shop at three o'clock."

Chapter 30

Sinclair, Josh, and Laura squeezed themselves into a booth at the coffee shop, away from traffic, in one of the back corners and ordered their meal. They started spreading their notes and papers around the table. As beverages came and sandwiches arrived, piles of notes would be maneuvered to make room for the food. Sinclair asked, "When you went through the notes, Laura, what did you find?"

"We had already talked to the three in New York. They knew we'd made the connection about the tattoo before the man in Iowa died. It doesn't matter whether we'd talk to the professor, since he was the next victim."

The FBI agent pounded his fist on the table and said, "Damn."

"What's the matter boss?" mocked Josh.

"I was hoping we hadn't gotten to one or two."

"What difference would it have made?" wondered detective Miles.

"The killer stopped putting the tattoo right in front of our faces, so it has to be someone we'd already shown our cards to. I guess this doesn't help eliminate anyone." Sinclair stuffed part of a burger in his mouth and then asked, "Dunbar. What did you come up with on our suspects' alibis?"

Dunbar finished a sip of cola and then responded, "The black man was at the diner the whole time. The cops doing the stakeout said he never leaves. He's always either working the place or upstairs in his apartment."

"What about our publisher?"

"The guys shadowing him are about as awake as the Chicago guys. Mr. Miller went on a religious retreat in upstate New York, somewhere in the mountains. It was a three or four day thing."

Laura chimed in with, "So that means he's not the killer, right?"

Josh said, "Unfortunately, no. The cops figured this place was far enough away and since it had only one or two roads leading to it, figured they could stay down at the bottom watching the main road. All they could say was the man's car never came out during the time he was there."

Sinclair mumbled through the food in his mouth, "Did anyone there with him vouch for his whereabouts?"

Josh enjoyed watching the mighty FBI agent slowly fall apart in front of his eyes. The man who just a few weeks ago was cocky and invincible, was becoming worried and desperate. Speaking with food in his mouth would have been a grievous faux pas earlier in the case. Josh told him, "You know, there are these handy little devices called napkins, don't you?"

"Just shut up and tell me more."

"We talked to the people who run the retreat and they can't swear he was there all the time either."

"Why the hell not?" asked Sinclair while spraying food from his mouth.

"They said the whole purpose of the retreat is solitude. They said something about atonement or purification, but anyway, each person gets a cabin and then they're left alone. They know he got there and they know he left. They can't swear what he did in between."

Lewis wiped his hands on a napkin, ranting, "And because the surveillance team wasn't checking every vehicle in and out of there, our guy could have left, done the professor, and still gotten back in time. What about that Fingers guy?"

"He was on a ski trip in Vermont. The team watching him did a better job of keeping tabs on him. He was there the entire time, but I don't think it means he's clean."

Laura wanted to know, "Why doesn't that clear him?"

Josh pointed out, "This guy claims to be connected with the Mafia or at least he acts like it. Why couldn't he have ordered one of his boys to do the murder?"

"He's got a point," said Laura.

"No, he doesn't have a point," chided the FBI agent. "These murders have been personal. There's no way the killer isn't doing it himself."

Josh became aggressive with his answer, "How in the hell do you know? You said yourself things have changed. Whoever snuffed the professor didn't care about the tattoo. Who's to say Carletti knew we were watching and instead of doing it himself, had one of his boys do it, and the guy just botched the tattoo part of it?"

"You're forgetting two important things. First, the killer had to get into the building. Who in their right mind would let one of those goons in? Second, the murder was way too complicated for a Mafia hit. They put a bullet in the back of your head. It's quick and effective. Besides, which one of Carletti's men is bright enough to figure out the deep-freeze technique?"

Josh felt indignant when he said, "Hey, I'm just offering my ideas."

"Well do us all a favor and keep them to yourself. I'm putting money on the Jew. He's the key to this whole thing."

Laura tried to defuse the anger between the two men, changing the subject, by asking, "Regardless who we think did it, we've got to do something before another one dies."

"Frankly, I say we wait and arrest the last one left standing," said a disgusted Inspector Dunbar.

The FBI agent stood up, tossed some money on the table, and said, "That's the most intelligent thing you've said in weeks. I'm going to my room. You two make sure the officers in New York have tightened their surveillance. Tomorrow, we'll fly there and lean on the Jew. I'll make the son of a bitch crack. He did it and I'm going to nail his butt."

After Sinclair left the room, Laura said, "You know Josh, you don't always have to push the man."

"Are you defending him?"

"I wouldn't call it defending him. He's just trying to do his job and you're always pushing his buttons to get a rise out of him."

"You're damned right I am. I've had his mister perfect bullshit ever since Iowa. Someone needs to take him down a notch."

Laura seemed to have mixed emotions when she quietly said, "Yeah, I know what you mean. I wouldn't mind being there when he falls on his face."

"I'm not so sure you're telling the truth."

"What are you saying?"

Josh pushed deeper with, "I've been watching you two today. Is there something going on here I should know about?"

"I don't know what you're talking about."

"The hell you don't. All of a sudden he's calling you by your first name. I've seen you look at each other like there's a dirty little secret. So what gives?"

Laura replied, "I didn't know it when he had you sent on that errand last night, but he asked me to dinner at the fancy restaurant on the roof."

"Oh, so that's it."

Laura resented the insinuation, even though it wasn't far from the truth. "It isn't what you think. I didn't know he'd set you up. I even asked why you weren't there."

"What did he say?"

Laura looked down before sheepishly saying, "You really don't want to know?"

"That's where you're wrong. I really do want to know."

"He said something about wasting such a meal on an unrefined baboon such as yourself."

She was surprised Josh didn't explode at the comment. Josh sat calmly and said, "That's what I'd expect him to say. So what was the meal about?"

"You know, I'm not really sure. We got to talking about his time in Paris and drinking wine. The next thing you know, it was late and we went to his suite."

Now, Josh started to explode, "You went up to his suite? I'll kill the son of a bitch."

"Nothing happened."

"That's not the issue. The question is whether or not you wanted something to happen."

Laura pointed out, "You and I are not husband and wife, you know. I've never heard you talk about permanence. I'll admit, there are some things about the guy that are attractive."

"Like what?"

"He's traveled, polite, refined, and a gentleman. I thought he was different than you."

"Thanks a lot."

"See! That's what I mean. You men are all alike. You're all a bunch of cavemen. You drag your knuckles on the floor and piss on the wall to mark your territory. Now you're out there pounding your chest, telling the world to stay away because this is my woman."

"So you're saying you wanted him!"

"Not only that, Einstein. I was about ready to give myself to him when you knocked on the door last night."

The way Laura matter of factly blurted out the information, took Josh by surprise. He sat silent with a shocked look on his face. Laura let him stew on her words for as long as he wanted. Dunbar took a deep breath and then asked, "So, that's the way it is, huh?"

"Is what, the way it is?"

"I mean, you're dumping me for him?"

Laura decided he had suffered enough from the brutal way she hit him earlier. "You didn't hear what I said. I was about ready to give myself. I didn't."

Josh wasn't necessarily comforted by her statement when he asked, "What are you saying?"

"Look. I'm a big girl now and you are not the only man on this planet. Maybe something will become of us, but for now, you don't own me. Last night I got wrapped up in his stories of Paris and had a little bit too much to drink."

"What changed your mind?"

"When you knocked at the door, it shocked me out of my fantasy and I had a chance to see him for what he was. I didn't mean anything to him. I was just another notch on his reputation."

"So you decided you wanted me over him?"

"Don't go stupid on me, Josh. I didn't choose you over him. I chose not to sleep with him, for what he was and not what I thought he was."

"I guess I'm not seeing the difference here."

Laura said, "I've been watching him fall apart the past couple of weeks. This case isn't going well for him and it threatens to ruin his perfect record with the Bureau. The rougher things get, the rougher his edges get. Underneath the polished exterior is a man who is getting worried."

"I thought I was the only one seeing it."

"You two guys are the same. The difference is, you don't put on a show to cover it. He does. For a while there, I was impressed by his record and his appearance, but last night really woke me up."

Josh lowered his anger a notch or two and said, "Look. I'm sorry I jumped on you a second ago."

"Hey, that's okay. I have a hunch I'd have been sorrier if I'd slept with him."

Josh wanted to know, "Did you tell him about us?"

"Of course not. It's none of his business and it had better stay that way. I want to be there when we collar the killer. If he knew about us, he'd ship one or both of us out of here in a heartbeat. "

"So, where do we stand?"

"On the murder case?"

Josh laughed a bit and said, "Yes, on the murder case, but us too."

"As far as we're concerned, I'll admit to almost making a mistake last night if you admit you learned a lesson today."

"That's a deal. Now what about the murder case?"

Laura admitted, "I think he's going in the wrong direction, but it's his show. Since he doesn't know about us being an item, let's use it to our advantage."

"What are you saying?"

"I'm saying we work together for ourselves. If we nail the killer, we can make sure to get our share of the fame. If Sinclair blows it, we can make sure he takes the whole fall. Frankly, I'm getting bored with this whole thing. I'd rather get back to California and some normal murders."

Josh laughed again, agreed to the deal, and then asked jokingly, "So, if I talk French to you, will you sleep with me tonight?"

Chapter 31

Laura asked Dunbar, "How many more days until he cracks?"

"I don't know. He's been pretty stable the past week or so, but when he gets a load of this, it might send him over."

The scene outside of the Harlem diner was chaotic. The police had sectioned off the street for half a block on either side. Still, there was a huge mob of people on the street for so late at night. The police lights flashed around the dirty, run-down buildings. A dozen different soul tunes filled the air from the windows. A hundred curious faces peered from the windows, wondering what happened in their neighborhood eatery.

When Sinclair pushed his way through the ring of officers holding back the crowd, he stumbled into the open street. The tails of his open trench coat flailed through the air. In the middle of the lighted ring, the scene looked more like a bullfight than a crime scene. Harried and irritated, he walked up to his two teammates and demanded, "How in the hell did this happen?"

Josh shrugged his shoulders and said, "Nobody seems to know."

"What do you mean? Where was the surveillance team?"

"They were in the diner having a cup of coffee. One minute Mr. Williams is waiting on them, the next minute he's dead."

Sinclair was raging, "I want to see those officers, now!"

"We sent them home," answered Laura. "They were pretty shook up by what happened and what they saw.

Besides, there were other people in the diner as well. None of them saw what happened."

Sinclair kicked at a chair, sending it sliding across the room. "Damn it. We've only got three people to watch and still someone gets killed. So what did happen?"

"According to the witnesses," Josh related, "Mr. Williams was serving the customers and cooking in the kitchen. I guess when it's late and there are few customers, he does all the work himself until no one else is left to serve. Then he closes the place."

"So how'd he get killed?"

"The police officers said, they'd just ordered some eggs from him. He goes out back to fix them. When he didn't return, the officers went into the kitchen to find him. They found him dead."

"No one in the diner heard or saw anything?"

Josh pointed at the pick-up and order window as he said, "They couldn't see anything because the only view into the kitchen is from that little window. It's behind the counter and pretty high, so someone would have had to be standing right in front of it to see anything in the kitchen."

"Didn't they hear anything?"

Laura replied, "Nobody heard anything they thought was unusual. This is a diner, and no one thought banging pots and pans was abnormal."

"There's a billion people a day through here, so looking for fingerprints would be useless," added Josh.

Laura chimed in with, "Besides, we've never found prints at the other murder scenes."

Sinclair rubbed his hand over his face, through his hair, and then huffed, "Fine. So where's the body and how did he die?"

Josh flipped his notebook shut and put his pen into his shirt pocket. He pushed open the swinging door into the kitchen and said, "Sinclair, I think you should see this yourself."

The trio walked into the kitchen. Tables and various cooking appliances lined both sides of the long galley. There were refrigerators, cutting boards, frying grills, and large vats for deep-frying food. In front of the largest fry pot, lay the body of Leroy Williams. He was wearing his normal blue jean pants and a cooking apron without a shirt. Everything looked normal from the neck down.

From the neck up, he was a swollen brown and burned mass. Sinclair leaned down to get a closer look and then asked his teammates, "Is that what I think it is?"

"Sure is," answered Josh. "The man's head has been batter-dipped, then deep fat fried to a crisp. The officers found him still bubbling away when they went looking for him."

"What a way to go," replied the FBI agent.

Being a redneck at heart, Josh couldn't resist throwing in, "I knew black people loved fried food, but this is a bit ridiculous."

Sinclair didn't appreciate the joke and yelled, "I'm tired of everyone screwing around on this case. If you can't keep your mind on the work, get your ass out of here!"

Josh gestured for him to back off and then said, "Calm down man before you burst a vein or something. I was just trying to lighten things up a bit. Besides, look at the bright side. This man is dead, which leaves us only two other suspects."

Sinclair's mind cleared a bit and he asked, "That's right. So, do we know where Carletti and Miller were tonight?"

Laura had the notes in her hand and read, "Miller was home all night. At the time of the murder, the stakeout people could see him clearly in his living room watching television."

"What about Carletti?"

"Carletti initially claimed to have been in his office all night."

"Did our people confirm it?"

"No. According to them, he somehow got into a car without them knowing and went out, just about the time of the murder. They tried to follow him, but got lost in traffic about ten blocks from here."

Sinclair raised his hands into the air and said, "Yes, there is a God! So, did we confront him with this information?"

"Yes, I did and he changed his story. He claimed he was going to a restaurant. He got there, but the time the restaurant says he arrived, was after the murder took place."

Sinclair started to head for the door of the diner, smiling and saying, "I knew he was the one. Let's get over there and see what our gangster friend has to say now."

Laura was confused when she asked, "Did I miss something? We thought you were sure it was Miller doing the killings."

"At first, he was my primary suspect. With this new information, I'm sure Carletti's the one. He sneaks out. He lied to you about it and he's in the general neighborhood at the right time. Let's go nail him."

When they got to the office of Fingers Carletti, the guards outside put up no resistance. The officers were ushered directly into his personal and opulent office. As the trio entered the room, Carletti said, "Welcome. Have a seat. I've been expecting you."

"Why?" asked Sinclair. "Did you do something which would raise our interest?"

"Not at all," answered a calm but worried Carletti. "When I heard about the untimely demise of my good friend Brownie and the fact that I happened, by sheer coincidence, to be passing by his neighborhood, I figured it was just a matter of time before you'd drop by to ask me some questions."

Josh asked, "You don't seem too worried about it?"

"An innocent man has nothing to fear in America. If I am worried, it's because I may be the next attempted victim."

"So you're saying you had nothing to do with the murder of Mr. Williams?" inquired the FBI agent.

Carletti leaned forward and lit a big, fat cigar and then gestured with an outstretched palm, "Ask the men you had following me. We drove from here, directly to Anthony's for dinner. The traffic was really bad, but we never stopped and we were never in Harlem."

"We checked with the restaurant and found out you didn't arrive there until well after the murder. You had time to go to the diner and kill him," pressed Sinclair.

"I told you the traffic was very bad. The men following me can vouch for how long it took to get there."

Sinclair said, "Our men got separated from you in traffic."

Carletti started to get a bit more nervous when he replied, "Well I'm sorry your men got lost. I assure you, I had no reason to kill Brownie. Personally, I liked the man."

Laura asked Fingers, "Did Mr. Williams ever come to you for money?"

"Yes, he did. His diner was getting behind on paying the bills. I loaned him some money, but it was a regular business deal. He paid me back, with interest. There's nothing wrong with that."

Sinclair pressed him with, "There is if you were using it as pressure to get him to cut you in on his share of the tontine."

Carletti froze for a second and then said, "I don't know what you're talking about."

"The hell you don't. We know all about the tontine. You all served together in the war. You all got those tattoos. You stayed in touch through the newsletter. The whole reason you did it was to keep track of when each of you died. Isn't that right?"

Carletti was feeling the pressure a bit when he replied, "So what? We were war buddies. A lot of guys stay in touch with their old units."

Josh took his turn at weighing in with, "We know about the tontine. We know the bank in Paris is keeping something for the last one of you who is alive. It must be pretty valuable for someone to kill for it."

"I don't know what you're talking about. Look around here. What would Brownie have that I would want?"

Sinclair rejoined, "He's alive and that keeps you from collecting on the tontine. I think you've been killing these people one at a time. I think you tried to lean on Brownie to sign over his share in exchange for his life. When he didn't, you killed him."

"That's a great story. It's also ridiculous. Why me and not the Jew boy?"

"Mr. Miller has an alibi for tonight. You don't," offered Laura.

Carletti started to heat up, "I got a dozen people who will vouch for where I was tonight and any other night someone got snuffed. I have no need for money."

Sinclair pried, "You didn't necessarily have to do the murders. You could have ordered them done."

"Okay, so I put on the airs of a big wheel, but I've got no reason to be killing these guys. I'm a legitimate business man. It's the Jew boy you need to be following. He's been trying to get his hands on it every since we found it. It's that money-loving Jew you need to nail, not me."

Josh saw his opening and asked, "What is the 'it' you're talking about? What does the last surviving man get?"

"It's some gold and jewel-covered cup. We found it and couldn't decide how to split it up. A friend of ours in France told us about these tontine things and we all agreed to it."

"No one had second thoughts?" asked Josh.

"No one but the Jew. He wanted to melt the gold down, sell the jewels, and divide the money. He's the one you need to be getting. In fact, he's the one you need to be protecting me from."

Sinclair liked the game going on. "Why? Are you getting a bit worried?"

"Normally, I'd say no. I got my people to protect me, but if they can get to the Professor and Brownie while the cops are guarding them, who knows."

Sinclair backed off and took a different approach. "I still think you did it. You've got no alibi for tonight and you've already expressed a dislike for Mr. Miller. I think you're the killer. I just can't prove it. Yet."

"You got me pegged wrong, G-man. It's the Jew you got to worry about. He's wanted to get his greedy hands on the cup from the first day we found it. You've got to protect me from him."

The FBI agent was satisfied with what he had for the moment. He said to Fingers, "Here's what I'm going to do. I'll let you think about it for a bit. If you're the killer, I'll just wait until you snuff Mr. Miller and then nail your butt. If you're right and he kills you, then I'll nail him.

The choice is yours. Admit to the murders and serve ninety-nine to life, or wait until Mr. Miller gives you a death sentence. We're leaving."

The three officers got up to leave. As they were walking out the door they heard Carletti saying, "I didn't do it. It's that Jew boy."

Twenty minutes later, they were knocking on the door of Jerome's house. The door opened and a sleepy Mr. Miller asked, "What's the matter officers? Do you want to come in?"

Sinclair was in the lead and answered, "There's no need for us to come in. We've just stopped by to tell you Mr. Williams was killed tonight at his diner in Harlem."

"That's terrible. Why are you bothering me? I was here all night."

Laura let him know, "We know you were, Mr. Miller. The police we had watching your home confirmed you were here all night. We actually think someone else did it."

"The only other one left is Carletti. I told you it was probably Fingers."

"We talked to him and he thinks you did it," offered Sinclair.

"But I was here all night. Besides that, why would I do it?"

"He did tell us about the gold and jewel-covered cup. He claims you've been trying to get it since the day you all found it."

"I resent his accusations. He's never liked me and I suppose I can say I never liked him either. Are you sure you wouldn't rather come inside?"

Josh and Laura started to move forward, but Sinclair blocked their path, saying to Jerome, "No. It's late. We can continue this discussion later. We just wanted you to know."

"I appreciate that. Damned shame. What a horrible way to go."

The door began to close, when the Jew's statement sunk in to Sinclair. He grabbed the door, preventing it from closing, and asked, "Why did you say it was a horrible way to go? We didn't tell you how he died."

Without hesitating, Jerome replied, "I just assumed he died a horrible death like the others you showed me. Even if it wasn't, being killed for money is a horrible way to go."

Sinclair released the door and let Miller go inside. The three walked down the block a few doors, then stopped to discuss what had happened. Josh asked, "Did you hear him about the murder?"

Laura wondered, "Do you think he knew how Brownie died?"

Sinclair declared, "He isn't the one. His explanation made perfect sense to me. It's Carletti who's the killer."

Josh defended Laura's question with, "Why would he say it was a horrible way..."

"I said drop it. Carletti is the killer, and here's what we're going to do. We've only got two suspects to cover now, so we do this personally. I'm going to take charge of covering Carletti. You two keep tabs on Jerome here."

"Why don't we leave this stakeout work to the local police?" asked Josh.

"Because we've gotten burned twice by them. You two keep the car and I'll get a cab back to the FBI office. I'll get another car and someone to help me." Sinclair looked around and after a minute or two hailed down a cab. After he got inside, he said, "I'm going to nail Carletti this time."

Josh looked at Laura and said, "He seems to be handling this pretty well."

"Yeah, right. He's so obsessed with the other guy, he didn't even hear what Miller had to say. I think he's wrong. Carletti isn't the man. Personally, I think Sinclair has finally gone over the edge."

Josh reasoned, "Hey, look at it this way. If he's right, he gets the glory and we can go home. If he's wrong, we get the glory and we can go home to gloat. We've got nothing to lose."

"You know I didn't look at it that way. You're right."

Dunbar reached into his pocket to find the car keys. He pulled out an empty hand and screamed, "That son of a bitch drove off with the keys to the car!"

Chapter 32

Josh sat in the driver's seat of their car, outside of the jewelry store. He could clearly see Jerome working behind the counter. The store was closed, but there was work to do none the less. Every night it was the same routine.

Josh's eyes began to wander from the storefront, to Laura's front. Slowly he lowered his hand from the steering wheel and reached across the seat, to where Laura was trying to get some sleep. Gently he placed his hand on Laura's knee. She didn't shoo him away, so he slowly started to slide up the hem of her dress. "Can't you keep your mind on your work?" asked Detective Miles.

Josh retracted his hand as if he'd touched a hot stove. "It's not my fault. We've been living in this car for ten days now. Every day it's the same thing. Miller gets up and opens the store. He works there all day with one of us standing in the store, while the other one grabs some shut-eye."

"I know. The store closes and then he spends a few hours sitting behind his desk doing paperwork, before he eats dinner and goes to sleep. If he was trying to lull us into a sense of false security, he's doing a good job."

Josh shifted around in his seat so he could face her better. "I still think Sinclair's full of it. Carletti is not the killer. This guy is and he knows we're watching him. He's going to wait for us to give up and go away."

"That isn't going to happen. Sinclair will wait until hell freezes over before he gives up."

Josh returned his hand to her knee, saying, "Wouldn't a bit of a diversion be nice?"

She took his hand and moved it a few inches up her thigh, asking, "A diversion for whom?"

Josh leaned forward to kiss her, but stopped a few inches short of his target. "I suppose if we do this right, it will be a diversion for both of us."

The two began to kiss, slowly and gently. They had all night, so there was no rush. The large, black sedan provided ample space to move around, and the bench-type front seat posed no obstacle like some of the newer cars, with bucket seats.

Laura arched her head back as he kissed the edge of her jaw near her ear. Quietly Josh nibbled briefly on her ear lobe before taking advantage of her exposed neck. He softened the pressure of his kiss to allow air to seep around his lips and blow gently on the tiny hairs of her skin. He headed down the side of her nape until he reached the little triangle which forms between her collar bone and the muscles of her neck.

Josh's tongue flicked out to tickle the spot and small goose bumps started to form on her skin. When he buried his mouth into the crevice and gently chewed the sinews under the skin, the goose pimples flowed down her body causing Laura to pull his head deeper into her body. He felt the air flow deeply into her lungs and then drift back out in a long drawn out sigh of, "Oh my!"

When her grip lessened, he changed the direction on his kiss and headed back to the center of her neck, blowing his hot breath across her small Adam's apple. He deftly swirled his tongue through the depression where Laura's neck met her breastbone. He knew she particularly loved that spot being kissed.

Laura shifted slightly, placing her back closer to the door and lowering their bodies a bit. This shift in position caused Josh to slide further down on her body, to where his lips were now hovering above her cleavage. The scent of her perfume filled his nose and made him a bit heady. She reached down to help him by slipping open the top two buttons of her blouse. The lacy edges of her bra cups peeked out of the parting lapels.

Not that he needed any incentive, but Laura's other hand had found its way to his side. She slid it down past his belt, until with her palm up, she cold feel the tautness in the front of his thigh. Leaning forward as he was, the muscles were stretched and tight to support their weight. It provided a perfect surface to slide inward in search of what she hoped was an interested party. The landmark was not hard to find.

One of his hands had found its way up under the hem of her dress and he began stroking her thighs. The stockings provided some texture to her normally milky thighs. As he neared the top, the texture thickened into lace at the hem of her thigh high hose. "Damn, I love how you hate pantyhose."

Laura whispered into his ear, "Normally it's cooler, but at times like this it makes things hotter." She felt his fingers dance across the hose tops and tickle the clasp of her garter belt. She also felt the growing dampness in her panties and the growing moist spot on Josh's pants. She cooed, "They seem to be working their magic."

Josh buried his head in her breasts and noticed her bra closed in the front. He fished a finger into the fray and unclasped her bra. The weight of her breasts, aided by gravity and the elastic of the cups pulled open the front of her blouse. The cool air rushed across her now exposed nipples, instantly erecting them and causing a chill to flood across Laura's body.

Laura returned the favor and unzipped his trousers. She fished a finger through the fly in his boxer shorts and pulled out Josh's best friend. He stiffened at her touch, both in her hand and over his body.

His reflex was to slide a hand along the back of her thigh, scooping under her to grab a satin covered cheek in his palm. Josh started to tighten his grip when the radio crackled, "Team one to team two. Do you read me?"

Laura startled and hit her head on the car's side window. "Damn him to hell!" she screamed out.

Panting, Josh sat up and tried to compose himself. He said, "It's like that guy knows when I'm trying to have a little bit of fun."

The radio repeated, "Team one to team two. Are you there?"

Josh took a couple of deep breaths and then keyed the microphone saying, "This is team two. Go ahead." Laura started reassembling her clothes, while Josh raised his palms in a gesture of exasperation.

"This is Sinclair. How is the pigeon on your end?"

Josh looked over at the jewelry store, but had to wipe some of the steam from the window before he could see the Jew sitting behind his desk working away. "There's no change on our end. What about your end?"

"There's no change here. You can go back to what you were doing. Team one, over and out."

Josh and Laura looked at each other for a second and then broke out laughing at Sinclair's comment. Josh zipped his pants and said, "Hell, I don't think I could get it up for fear he'd call again."

Laura tilted the rearview mirror to see if she was still in one piece. She pushed her hair around for a second, checked her make-up, touching up her lips a bit before saying, "That could make you swear off sex forever."

Josh finished wiping the windshield clean of condensation and saw the jeweler behind his desk. A thought came to him and he asked, "What would prevent us from asking Mr. Miller to dinner?"

She looked across the street and thought for a second before answering, "Why would you want to do it?"

"We're supposed to keep tight surveillance on this guy right?"

"Yeah."

"How much tighter can we get than having dinner with him?"

"I suppose, but I don't get your point."

"I'm sick to death of sandwiches, donuts, and coffee in this car every night. Wouldn't you like to sit down to a normal meal for a change?"

Laura gestured by hitting her head with a hand and said, "That's an obvious answer. Of course I would."

"I've been dying to ask him some questions of my own. Look, we can kill two birds with one stone. We get dinner and can ask some questions without Sinclair around. Why not?"

Laura opened the car door and grabbed her purse. She didn't wait for Josh as he stumbled out of the car trying to catch up with her. She went to the front door of the store and knocked. Miller looked up. He saw who it was and came over to open the door. “What can I do for you, officer?”

By now, Josh had caught up. Laura said, “My partner and I were just wondering if you might like to join us for dinner tonight. How about it?”

“I thought that was against regulations or something.”

Josh offered, “We're supposed to keep an eye on you. We can do it and eat at the same time. Besides, what better protection could you have than to be with two police officers?”

He thought about it for a minute and then Jerome reached for his hat and coat hanging next to the door. He switched off the lights of the store and said, “You are absolutely right. Let's go.” As they cleared the doorway, Jerome turned around to lock the door. He put on his hat and coat. He then asked, “Where do you want to eat?”

Laura looked at Josh who shrugged his shoulders. She turned back to Jerome and said, “This is your neighborhood. You pick the place.”

The Jew pointed up the block and said, “There's a good Kosher place around the corner. You don't mind do you?”

Laura nodded for him to lead and the trio walked off in search of food. When they arrived, Josh was somewhat disappointed to see it was a delicatessen. He grabbed Laura by the arm and whispered into her ear, “Just what I need, another sandwich.”

Laura asked Jerome, “No offense, but we were thinking more along the lines of a regular restaurant. We've just about had our fill of sandwiches.”

The Jew laughed and shaking his head said, “You meshuganas are all alike. You think a deli is just for pastrami sandwiches. You leave this to me and I'll show you what a real Jewish feast is. You guys are buying. Aren't you?"

They went inside and sat down at a table far away from the front door. Jerome ordered the meal. Speaking in Yiddish, they couldn't understand anything he said. The food arrived. Josh looked at a few items and turned his nose up at their appearance. Jerome saw his reaction and said, "Trust me. Just give it a try. You'll like it."

Josh stuck a spoon into what appeared to be soup and tentatively tasted the concoction. "Hey. This isn't bad," he said. He took a second, more confident spoonful and then said, "In fact, this is really good." Jerome started to tell him what he was eating, but Josh cut him off saying, "No. Don't tell me what's in it. I don't want to know."

Laura had just finished tasting some meat. She asked, "This is delicious. What is it?"

"It's mutton. Sheep meat. You like it?"

"It's wonderful."

The time passed quickly. As the hours passed, the barriers between the two officers and the suspect began to lower. They didn't completely trust each other, but they shared some common ground in their mutual dislike of the FBI agent. The Jew said, "That agent is a putz. He pushes and pushes."

"You should work with him day after day," commented Josh.

"We should have done this weeks ago," said Laura to Jerome. "The story of how you guys found the cup is amazing. What's the thing worth?"

Jerome suddenly got serious. He'd been freely offering stories about the war and the tontine, as the officers already knew about those facts. This last question of Laura's hit a little closer to home. He took a couple of deep breaths and then swallowed a big gulp of water.

Laura saw his change in expression and told him, "Look. We don't care about the cup. That's your business. We want the person who's been committing the murders. If you're the last one left after we take him to jail, you can have the cup."

"No. That's not the problem. I've spent so many years avoiding any discussions about it. Actually, it feels good to finally share this with someone. I didn't realize how much this burden was weighing on my conscience."

Laura placed her hand on Jerome's and repeated, "When you are the last one left, the cup is yours. You deserve it."

Jerome puzzled, "You make it sound like you're pretty sure someone else is doing the killing. Your boss doesn't seem to agree. He thinks I'm the one."

Josh and Laura looked at each other and then Josh said, "I know how you got that idea, but that's old news now. Sinclair changed his mind. He actually thinks Carletti has been doing the killing. The whole reason we were assigned to you, is he wants to be there when they nail Carletti. The fact is, I was the one who thought you were the killer."

"I take it you've changed your mind as well."

"Not one hundred percent, but my gut tells me you're not the one."

Jerome was a bit confused, but took the officer at his word. He turned to Laura and asked, "What was it you wanted to know?"

"How valuable is this cup?"

"It depends upon who you want to believe. As far as I'm concerned, it is only worth the gold and jewels. "

Josh asked, "You make it sound as if someone disagrees with you. Is there some other opinion?"

"When we found the cup, we showed it to a French woman we knew. She told us it was a priceless piece of artwork. She called it the Chalice of Justice. She claimed it came over with King Arthur or something. It was her threat of turning us in for destroying the treasure, which forced us into making the pact. I wanted to break it up and melt it down."

Laura wondered, "Did you believe her?"

"I didn't then, but I've been able to research it a bit, and she may be correct. I'm still inclined to take it apart and sell it in pieces."

"Why?"

"It could be hard to explain where I got it. Even if they believed me, there's likely to be a fight between the French government, the Germans, and maybe even the English or something. It could be tied up for years. I might die before I'd see any money from it."

Josh asked, "If you broke it apart and sold it, what would it be worth?"

Jerome sat pensively for a second and then replied, "You have to remember I haven't seen it for twenty plus years. As I recall what was on it, if I sold the pieces a bit at a time, behind the scenes to collectors and avoided taxes and such, it could easily bring a million dollars."

There was silenced shock at the enormity of the prize awaiting the last survivor. Laura thoughtfully said, "No wonder someone is willing to kill for it."

After a few more minutes of reflection, Jerome asked the two officers, "Do you think your boss knows?"

Laura snapped out of her shock and said, "No. He knows it is a jewel covered gold cup, but he doesn't know it's worth a million bucks."

"I suppose you're going to have to tell him," implied the Jew.

Josh reluctantly said, "I suppose we do. Why?"

Jerome apparently thought he could trust these two and said, "My biggest fear throughout this whole thing has been the FBI. I'm telling you I'm not the murderer. Whether you believe me or not, I've just been counting on being the last survivor. I didn't want to tell the agent anything for fear the FBI would try and take the cup away from me."

"That sounds like a valid concern, now that you mention it," agreed Josh. "Why are you telling us?"

"My religion teaches us that men need their friends, especially in times of great need. Maybe we can be friends to each other in our time of need."

Laura was curious as to where this conversation was going and asked, "What are you suggesting?"

"I need protection from whoever is doing these murders and I feel such services should not go unrewarded."

"Are you offering us a bribe?"

"Not exactly," said the Jew. "I'm just suggesting that if I am the last survivor, I could be appreciative to those who helped me along the way."

"Still sounds like a bribe to me," said Josh. He looked at Laura and could tell by the look on her face she agreed with him. Josh said to the Jew, "Like I said earlier. We could care less about the chalice. If you are the last one standing, it's yours. You deserve it. There's only two things we want and you might actually want to help us with them."

Jerome was curious now. "What is it you want?"

Laura answered, "We want to nail the killer so we can go home. This started out a simple, but interesting murder case, now it's a big bore."

"And what is the other thing you want?"

Josh wanted to answer this one and said, "We'd love to see the FBI agent fall on his face or at least end up with some egg on his face."

"How can I help you with that?"

Josh leaned forward and stated, "If Carletti is the killer, Sinclair will make the collar and try to grab all of the glory. If the three of us go to the press and say we told him months ago about Carletti, he'd have to explain why more people had to die before he caught him."

Jerome liked the idea, but asked, "What if Carletti isn't the killer?"

Laura now leaned forward to say, "That would make you the prime suspect. If we can prove it, Josh and I will nail you. We get the collar because Sinclair was fishing in the wrong pond."

"But I already told you I'm not the one."

"Even better," added Josh. "If you're clean, we walk away. Sinclair is left holding an empty bag and you're on your way to Paris to collect your prize."

"You'd really walk away?"

Laura replied, "Where we come from, a couple of extra unsolved murders, especially ones messed up by the FBI, are no big deal. We can go home and you can fly to Paris."

The three thought about it for a second and then started to laugh. The laughter kept building until the Jew said, "And I suppose if someone sent you both an anonymous gift in the mail, say some jewelry, who's to know?"

The trio walked back to the store, where Jerome headed upstairs to his home and the officers returned to their car. Josh put the key in the ignition to turn on the radio. Immediately it crackled out, "Headquarters to team two."

"This is team two. Go ahead, headquarters."

"Where have you been, team two?"

"We were eating dinner. Why?"

"Team one wants you to call him on a telephone at 586-1434."

"Team two, over and out."

Laura ran to a pay phone on the corner and dialed the number. Josh watched her animated conversation through the glass wall and the stark glow of the streetlight above. Laura hung up the phone and returned to the car. Josh asked her, "What did Sinclair want?"

"Carletti was killed less than an hour ago."

Shocked, Josh thought out loud, "The Jew was with us. That means he didn't do it. Who did?"

Laura got a sly look on her face and pointed out, "We can worry about it later. You realize Carletti got snuffed right under Sinclair's nose, don't you?"

Josh perked up, smiled, and started the car. "This I've got to see."

Chapter 33

The lights in the work yard of the concrete mixing plant were all switched on. It seemed almost as bright as daylight when Josh and Laura turned their car into the parking lot in front of Carletti's personal trailer office. As they got out of the car, one of the police officers on the scene asked, "Are you the two cops from California?"

Josh answered, "Yeah. Why do you ask?"

"Well, your boss is sitting over there and he ain't very happy. I thought you could use the warning."

They signaled their thanks and looked over to the end of the trailer. Sinclair sat on one of the planter boxes, his elbows on his knees and his hands holding up his bowed head. A cigarette was burning in the fingers of one hand. "I didn't think he smoked," commented Laura.

"Well, he does now," replied Josh.

The pair walked over to the FBI agent and stood in front of him for a minute. Finally, Josh could no longer restrain his amusement, nor his desire to gloat and asked, “So, did anything interesting happen here tonight?”

“Shut the fuck up. I was wrong. Is that what you wanted to hear?”

“It'll do for a start, but I was wondering how this could have happened right under your nose?”

“Cut it out, Josh,” chided Detective Miles. “You can gloat all you want later, but for now we've got a job to do.” Laura sat down next to the agent.

Sinclair looked up at her and said, “Thanks, but I suppose I've got it coming. Damn! Damn it all! Your partner's right. How could it have happened? I thought I had all the angles covered.”

Laura wanted to be more supportive, but inside she enjoyed seeing him humbled, so she stayed professional with her actions. “How did the killer get to Carletti?”

“I thought I had it all covered,” mumbled the FBI agent. “This damned thing has a secret room and a hidden exterior door. The man could have been coming and going all night long and we wouldn't have known it.”

“What do you mean by a secret room? You mean like a basement or something?” inquired Dunbar.

“Why don't the two of you go inside and see for yourselves?” Sinclair gestured half-heartedly toward the door and continued, “You'll see what I mean. I'm going to stay out here for a little while longer.”

Dunbar and Miles left their sulking federal agent and stepped into the trailer. Everything looked as it did the last time they'd visited Carletti in his office. The only difference was one section of bookshelves, hinged as a secret door. Sitting on a sofa nearby was a sobbing young lady. An officer explained, “This pretty thing found the body.”

Dunbar sat on one side of her and Laura sat on the other. The girl's hair was well made up, but what was once a fine make-up job was streaked with tears and smudged from rubbing. She was still sobbing into a handkerchief. Laura asked, "What is your name?"

Wiping the tears from her eyes, she replied, "My name is Alice Mayberry, but Fingers just calls me Princess."

Josh looked at Alice's clothes. She certainly was not a secretary, unless Fingers gave his dictation in bed. Alice was wearing a fancy lace and silk dressing gown, which barely closed in the front. Underneath, she wore a long silk negligee, whose material didn't leave much to the imagination.

Laura asked her, "I know this is tough and I promise not to ask you a lot of questions, but can you tell me how you found the body?"

"Sure. I came over here like I normally do. Fingers and I have this semi-regular schedule."

"Are you his girlfriend?"

"Well, I suppose you can call me that if you want, but I'm sure he has other girls, too. He keeps an apartment for me a few blocks from here. Sometimes he comes to visit me there, but the last few months, he's been having me come here."

Josh asked, "So he called and you came over. You walked in the front door and found him dead?"

"No silly. Fingers sent a car over to pick me up. I arrived exactly at eleven o'clock like he says and I go to the secret door out back and use the secret knock he taught me."

"Then he answers the door and lets you in?" wondered Laura.

"Yeah, normally he opens the door for me, but tonight he didn't. I knocked again, but there was no answer. I tried the door and it was unlocked. I walked in, nice as pie, figuring he's playing some sort of trick on me, but he ain't." She began to cry again as she thought of the scene. "I found him laying there, dead. I screamed and his boys came running in. That's all I know."

"Thank you, Miss Mayberry," said Laura as she stood up.

The two officers walked through the open door and into the secret room... a secret bedroom. A couple of other policemen were in the room as well. "Nice place, huh?" one of them asked.

Josh looked around at all of the fine linens, silk draperies hanging on the walls, all of the gold-plated light fixtures, and the fancy marble statues. "Yeah, right. A nice playpen, if you ask me."

The officer offered, "The stiff's over there on the bed. Poor bastard."

Josh and Laura saw Carletti's body laid out on the bed. He looked more or less asleep, until you looked at his face. When you did, you saw a mass of brown material which appeared to have bubbled out of his mouth and nose. The material was solid, but airy, like cotton candy. It made his head look like a mass of tumors or mushrooms. Laura asked the officers, "What is this stuff?"

"Expanding foam insulation. The stuff is really sticky. Comes in a can. You squirt it where you need it and it expands ten to twenty times its original size."

"Why would the killer squirt it on his face?" wondered Josh.

"Not on his face, in his face," responded the officer. "Whoever did this squirted it in the guy's mouth. The shit started expanding and filled his throat, mouth, and expanded out of his nose. The medical examiner hasn't been here yet, but you have to figure the guy suffocated. Nasty way to die if you ask me. There's nothing he could have done. That stuff is sticky and it just keeps growing and growing."

Josh and Laura didn't want to explain why this didn't shock them. Considering some of the other murders, this one was pretty tame. Josh did want to know, "Where's this secret door the girl was talking about?"

"Comes in off the bathroom. Come over here and I'll show you."

The door opened into the parking garage behind the trailer, but on the adjoining property. Laura said, "That's how he could get in and out without being seen. The trailer looks like it sits against a brick wall, but the wall is part of this parking garage."

Josh added, "Pretty slick, disguising the door as a big sign. You wouldn't know it was here. So, how did our killer get in?"

"Not a trace. No fingerprints. No jimmy marks on the door."

Josh was looking at the door's locking mechanism. "This thing only opens from the inside. The fake sign covers enough of the door that you couldn't pry it open if you wanted to. Fingers must have let the killer in."

The officer agreed, saying, "That's the way we figured it. The getaway was easy enough. We didn't know this door was here, so we weren't watching it. Whoever it was just ran back out here and into the night."

The group returned to the bedroom where Laura commented, "It looks like there was a struggle in here."

The officer said, "I thought that too, but I figure it happened after he got the crap squirted in his head."

"Yeah, I suppose you're right. Thanks for your time."

The officers asked, "You guys are taking this a whole lot better than the FBI agent."

"He has a whole lot more to lose than we do."

Josh and Laura walked back outside, where Sinclair was beginning to feel a bit better. He saw them coming over and asked them, "Can you see how we missed it?"

Josh offered the first answer, "As much as I'd love to gloat, I have to admit I wouldn't have thought of it."

Laura was second when she said, "You look a bit better than you did a few minutes ago."

Sinclair stamped out his cigarette and said, "I've had time to realize it wasn't my fault. I've also had time to realize this leaves the Jew as the killer."

"I hate to burst your balloon," related Dunbar, "but we were with Miller at the time of the murder."

"Yeah, I know that. You were sitting out front and he must have slipped out, killed Carletti, and slipped back in when you weren't looking."

Josh was getting angry and said, "You've got a hell of a lot of confidence in us."

Sinclair wasn't going to back off of Josh, saying, "You're damned right I don't. You've been a pain in the ass through this whole thing."

It was Josh who backed off, when he realized it was Sinclair's butt in the sling and not his own. He had a ridiculing tone to his voice when he told Sinclair, "This sorry pain in the ass has news for you. We weren't out front, sitting in our car. We were having dinner, with Mr. Miller, in a restaurant the entire time the murder was being committed. How do you like that?"

"You were doing what?"

Laura piled on with, "That's right. We decided to question him over dinner. We were with him from about eight until almost midnight."

Sinclair's face grew beet red and he exploded, "I'm not going to be upstaged by two second-rate cops from California. You're making this up to cover your own tracks. You fell asleep. That's why I couldn't get you on the radio. "

"You're full of shit," observed Detective Miles.

"No. That's it, isn't it? You two fell asleep. The Jew came over here, killed Carletti, and now you're making up this ridiculous story to cover your tracks. Well, it isn't going to work."

"What are you going to do?" demanded Josh.

"I'll tell you what I'm going to do. We're going to get in your car and I'm going to go over and arrest Miller for the murders. Then, I'm going to get you two brought up on charges for gross misconduct while on duty. I'm not going to take the fall for your incompetence."

Josh started to take off his coat to challenge the FBI agent to fight, but Laura got in between them. Instead, Josh yelled, "You're damned lucky there's a lady present or I would knock your block off. The only incompetent here, is you. You just won't admit it!"

"Don't hide behind the lady. If you want a piece of me, come and get it," hissed Sinclair.

It was Laura who brought calm to the situation. "Josh, put your coat back on. Let's go over to Mr. Miller's. He'll confirm our story and numb nuts here can eat crow."

"Oh, sure, like the Jew wouldn't say whatever he has to in order to save his ass."

Pointing at Sinclair, Laura warned, "And you, you sorry excuse for a man, if you don't watch your mouth, this lady will take your block off herself."

Sinclair realized he had to look up at Detective Miles. In her shoes, she was a couple of inches taller than he was. It might be a good fight, but it would quickly become two against one. Besides, he had bigger issues on his mind. He waved them off, saying, "Fuck you both. Let's get in the car and visit the Jew. He did it and I'm going to prove it."

Chapter 34

Sinclair yelled, "I'm tired of screwing around here! Carletti is dead. You are the last one alive, so you must be the murderer."

Jerome Miller was just as tired. He repeated, "I've told you a dozen times already. Last night, when this murder supposedly took place, I was having dinner with your partners here. They've even told you themselves. If you won't believe me, why won't you believe them?"

"Because I figure they'd do and say whatever to cover their own butts. For all I know, you three could be working together." There was a pause while Sinclair considered his accusations. His expression changed as a thought gelled in his mind. "Yeah. That's it. It's all very clear now. You three are going to split the money from that golden chalice."

Josh was about fed up with the accusations. He seethed, "You don't know what you're talking about. You're just trying to cover your own butt. Carletti was killed right under your nose and now you're grasping at straws trying to blame us."

Sinclair turned on Josh, "I'd watch my step if I were you."

Dunbar considered the threat to be hollow. "What the hell are you going to do to me?"

Sinclair returned to Jerome and asked, "From Carletti's description of the cup, I'm betting it's worth a hundred thousand dollars. You're the expert. That cup's worth a hundred thousand, isn't it?"

Jerome looked quickly at Josh and Laura. He read no reaction in their eyes, so he replied, "Sounds about right to me. For an FBI agent, you have a keen sense for jewelry." Laura choked back a giggle.

"See. What did I tell you," ranted Sinclair. "I figure the Jew keeps half and you two split the rest. That's more than each of you makes in a year, just for turning your back at the right time."

Josh was just about to jump into the fray, when Jerome went on the offensive. "First, my name is Jerome, or at least Mr. Miller. I will not let you keep referring to me as the Jew. I let my buddies use it as a nickname, because most of them were ignorant and didn't know any better. Besides, I counted them as friends. You, sir, are neither, so I expect you to call me by my name."

Sinclair wasn't going to be bullied and said, "I'll call you whatever I damned well please."

"Have it your way. You can call me what you want. You suspect me of murder and I expect you to pressure me, but accusing these two officers of being crooked is uncalled for."

Sinclair sat down and sarcastically said, "I would expect you to stand up for your accomplices. They're your only alibi. If they go down, you go down."

"And another thing, they are not my only alibi." Jerome pulled out a piece of paper and said, "I've taken the time to list out the dates of all these murders and where I was during each. For seven of them, I was here in New York and did not have time to get to California or wherever. Here's a list of people who can vouch for my whereabouts."

"No doubt another collection of cronies who will say whatever you tell them to keep you from the gas chamber and line their own pockets."

Miller pointed to one of the entries on his list and asked, "What about this one? When Sarge was killed in

San Francisco, I was in the hospital having my gall bladder out. Did I bribe the entire hospital?"

The color left Sinclair's face. This was apparently a detail he had missed or neglected to check. It was one of the earlier murders. He could feel his grip on the Jew slipping away, and with it his perfect FBI career. Jerome saw the reaction on the agent's face and said, "I didn't think you knew that one. You also didn't know that when Tinker was stuffed into the safe, I was in Israel with a group from our Temple."

Sinclair's shoulders fell. He thought to himself, "How could I have missed that? Was I so blinded by the process? Once I had the list of who was alive, I only checked the subsequent murders' alibis. Why didn't I check the older ones?"

Jerome dropped the note into the FBI agent's lap and returned to his seat. He said, "I really don't expect an apology, but I hope this finally puts the issue to rest. I'm not the killer you seek."

Sinclair turned to his two partners, trying to recover some of his dignity by attacking them. "Why didn't you two check these out? I always knew you two were incompetent. I don't know why I ever agreed to have you two along."

Josh could finally have his say, "You pompous, self-righteous, arrogant son of a bitch. For months now, I've listened to your insults. I've run your little errands and wild goose chases. Well, the birds have come back to roost and they are all crows. You screwed it up and I'm not going to let you palm it off on us."

Sinclair snapped back, "I didn't think you knew how to use words that big. Those were your cases. You two failed to check all of the alibis. It's not my fault."

"That's where you are wrong," retorted Dunbar. "We had just gotten the names on the list the morning you took over the case. You made it clear to her lieutenant that you were in complete charge of the case. No, I'm afraid you're the one holding the empty bag."

Sinclair stood and wanted to argue, but he was too angry and confused to do so. He decided a strategic retreat was in order. Sinclair turned to the Jew and said, "This thing isn't over yet. I know you did it. You did it for the money. It was always for the money. I can't prove it, yet, but this thing isn't over." With those parting words, Sinclair stormed out of the room and went outside the house to smoke a cigarette.

After the agent left, Jerome turned to the remaining two officers and asked, "Why didn't you tell him the chalice was worth a lot more?"

Josh said, "I think I'll save that one for later. Somewhere down the road, when I want to pull his chain, I'll call him up and tell him."

Laura wanted to know, "Personally, I'm satisfied you didn't kill those other men, but it brings up the question as to who did. Aren't you worried you could be next?"

"I suppose I am a little bit, but I've got some ideas along those lines."

"What are they?"

"I'm the only one who can collect on the tontine, so whoever it is certainly would not want me dead, at least if they are after the money. Somewhere along the way, they'll have to show themselves."

Josh asked, "Aren't you afraid they'll show themselves at the wrong end of a gun?"

"That's always a possibility and I'll just have to deal with it then. If the motive is the chalice, I'm banking on the fact that they need me alive to get it, but I don't think it's going to come down to it."

Josh and Laura looked at each other nervously as if they'd been duped by Jerome. It was Josh who probed the subject with, "You sound awfully sure of yourself, especially when you use the word 'if' when talking about the motives of the killer. Do you have some other idea as to what is really going on?"

"In fact I do. I think your boss was right all along."

Laura was in disbelief when she asked, "Carletti? You think Carletti is the murderer?"

"Yes, I do. I think he was killing those men off one at a time, or at least having someone kill them for him."

"Then who killed Fingers?" Laura asked.

"All of us in the tontine were sworn to secrecy. We didn't even tell wives or children. At least we weren't supposed to. My guess is someone told a relative, and they killed Carletti."

"I don't get it," said Dunbar.

"Oh, I'm not saying they told anyone about the chalice or the tontine. My hunch is that as the number of survivors dwindled, someone came to the same conclusion as Sinclair out there and left a note or something. You know, just in case something happened to them."

Laura said, "I never thought of that. You're saying someone figured Carletti was doing the murders and then killed him in revenge?"

"Exactly. I think Carletti was knocking us off, but someone like a friend of Brownie's figured it out and killed Fingers in his bedroom. Either way works for me."

Laura stood up and reached out a hand to Jerome. In it was a business card. He took the card and then shook her hand. She said, "Well, I hope you're right. If things change or you find out you're wrong, you can call me at this number in Los Angeles."

"I suppose I could send packages there as well?" Laura shook a finger at him and turned toward the door.

Josh pulled out his card and gave it to Jerome. The Jew took the card and said, "I'm certainly glad you two asked me to dinner last night. I'm curious. Why the sudden change of attitude?"

Josh thought about the interrupted necking session in the car and chuckled as he said, "You might say it was Sinclair's idea." A puzzled look appeared on Jerome's face. Josh saw it and said, "You know Sinclair is not going to let this drop."

"I know, but there's nothing for him to find. I didn't do it."

Josh followed Laura out the door and found Sinclair leaning against the car parked at the curb. He threw his cigarette to the ground and said, "Were you three figuring out how to divide the money?"

"Would you get off it," snapped Josh. "I have had enough of this case and more than enough of you. I'm going back to California. If you don't mind, I'll grab a cab."

"You might as well," mocked the FBI agent. "You're out of your league here." As Josh went to hail a taxi, Sinclair turned to Laura and asked, "What about you? You know, you might have a future in the FBI."

Laura turned toward the agent and asked, "I suppose you could make it a bit easier for me to get in?"

"You know we never did finish what we started the other night. You and I could continue working on this case. After all, I've got a perfect record to protect and I'm not going to let that clown from San Francisco ruin my reputation. While we're at it, I suppose we could discuss your getting into the bureau. I think I could make a pretty good case."

Laura slid a little closer to the agent and gently took the lapel of his coat in her hand. Stroking it, she looked hungrily into his eyes and then said, "I've got news for you. Your perfect record is already shot. " She released the lapel and slapped him across the face, which caught Josh's attention. As she stormed away from the agent, she yelled, “My case is one you will never solve.”

Laura walked over to where a cab had just pulled up in front of Josh. Dunbar was standing near the open door of the taxi, when Laura strode up to him and pushed him back against the cab, planting a big, deep, and wet kiss on his lips. Miles let go of him and climbed into the cab.

Josh, taken by surprise, needed a second or two to recover. When he did, his eyes met Sinclair's across the way. A big smile spread across Josh's face. He winked at the FBI agent, shrugged his shoulders, and gave Sinclair a mocking salute with his hand and an extended middle finger. Josh climbed into the taxi and it drove away, past the angry agent.

As they passed by, Sinclair shouted after them, “You two will regret it. This thing is far from being over.”

Chapter 35

The final confrontation

Jerome Miller labored up the stairs of the hotel, carrying the bulky and heavy wooden box. The bellman had offered to carry the parcel up to his room for him, but Jerome would have none of it. “Damn crazy French hotel,” he grumbled under his breath. “They can't have a normal elevator. No. They have to have some relic from the past which requires someone to operate it. Is the operator ever there when I need him? No. He's always off on some break or something.”

Nearing the fourth floor landing, he almost dropped the box, catching his grip at the last second. He sat the box on the floor and paused to wipe some sweat from his brow with a handkerchief. He picked up his precious cargo and started down the hall to his room. As he neared the intersection of the halls, the elevator arrived and opened onto his floor. "Damn him. Now he shows up."

A waiter rolled a tray off the elevator. On it was a bottle of champagne, sticking out from a silver bucket of ice. The waiter rushed past Jerome who called out, "I believe the champagne is for me."

The waiter stopped and said, "Pardon moi?"

"I said, I think the champagne is for me."

"I'm so sorry. Are you Monsieur Miller in the Emperor's Suite?"

Fumbling again with the box as he tried to find his key, he replied, "Yes. That's me."

"Allow me to help you monsieur." The waiter tried to take the box, but Jerome refused to let go of it. "As you wish, monsieur," responded the waiter who continued on his way toward Miller's room.

Jerome cradled the box on one knee, against the door jamb so he could unlock the door. As soon as the door opened, the waiter rushed past him and into the room. "Where would you like me to put this?"

"On the table over there will do fine."

"If there is anything else we may do for you, please do not hesitate to call."

Jerome's French was meager at best, but he had learned a few phrases which seemed to help. One was, "Merci. C'est pour vous." He stuffed a few bills of money into the waiter's hand as he rolled the cart out the door.

"God, I'm glad that ordeal is finally over," said Jerome in exasperation. He placed the box on the table next to the champagne bucket. He looked out the windows of his suite at the Paris skyline. The suite was large, luxurious, and cost far more than he really wanted to pay, but given the circumstances, it seemed to fit the moment.

He could hear the sounds of the street below him as they filtered through the open door of the balcony. Jerome walked over to the door the waiter had exited and made sure it was doubly locked before returning to the ancient box. He paused for a moment over the chest, before gently unlocking the clasp and opening the lid. The hinge creaked from age and rust. As he pulled off the black velvet cover, the light streaming in through the windows reflected off of the gold and jewels, dancing across his face.

"I've waited a very long time for you," he said lovingly. He pulled the chalice out of its case and talked to it as if it were a cherished, but long lost friend.

"I waited almost twenty-five years for this moment. All the time, praying I would be the one. Through all those years, I dreamed of this moment."

Jerome pretended the chalice was talking to him. "What's that you ask? Of course I've missed you. All those years you spent locked up in the dark, but now you are mine."

The Jew picked up a napkin and started to polish the cup, caressing its form and wiping off decades of age. "I waited through all of the unfortunate murders of my friends and then had to wait through another six months of that insufferable FBI agent. That is all behind us now. It's just you and me from now on."

He placed the chalice on the table and turned to the champagne bottle. He removed the foil wrapper from the neck and began to untwist the wires holding back the cork. From behind, he heard the sound of a heel landing on the polished wood flooring. Jerome turned to see a man entering the room from the balcony. It was a young man, a well dressed man. He was wearing gloves and holding a pistol in his hand. The gun was a small automatic pistol, with a silencer on the end. "Bon soir, Monsieur Miller," said the intruder.

It was time for another one of the few phrases Jerome knew. "Que diable voulez-vous?"

"Tres bien, Monsieur. Your French is pretty good for a Jew. I'll be more than willing to tell you what the devil I want, but for now, why don't you have a seat?" Using the muzzle of the gun, the intruder gestured toward one of the chairs. Jerome looked pensively for a second at the chalice and then decided to comply with the instructions. Gently he placed the champagne bottle back in the bucket, and then took a seat.

The intruder walked over to the telephone and pulled the cord from the wall. "I do not want us to be disturbed, while we get acquainted."

"Who are you?"

"You ask a very fair question. My name is Jean-Claude."

Jerome was sweating as he struggled to determine if he'd ever met this man before. He said, "I'm sorry, but I don't know you."

"If I told you my name was Jean-Claude Remarque, would you know me then?"

He searched his memory some more, but could not recall the name. "I'm sorry. I still don't remember. Have we done business or something in the past?"

The intruder chuckled as he walked over and took a seat near Jerome's. Jean-Claude commented, "You are a very funny man. Oui. You might say we've done business in the past. Maybe you'll remember my mother's name. Does the name Marie Remarque help you to remember?"

Suddenly, all the memories came flooding back to Jerome. His theories of the murders were swept aside by a possibility he could not have known, but one which now was threatening his life. "You are Marie's son? I didn't know she had a son."

"Make no mistake about it. I am her son and the whole point of this little drama is that none of you knew or even cared she had a son."

Jerome decided to be direct and asked, "So are you saying you've been killing off my friends?"

"Oui. C'est moi. I have been eliminating them one at a time."

"Why? What did we ever do to you?"

Jean-Claude calmly said, "Again, that is the point. None of you ever did anything to or for my mother. You American soldiers were all alike. You came to France and you took whatever you wanted, leaving behind whatever you did not. My mother considered you all as friends and you repaid her hospitality by abandoning her."

"What were we supposed to do?"

"I grew up without a father. After the war, my mother tried her best to keep the hotel open and make the ends meet, as you Americans say. Slowly, the hard work and the years of struggle took their toll. My mother's beauty faded into wrinkles and gnarled hands. All the time she would tell me how some day her American friends would come to help, as they promised."

Jerome countered with, "I don't ever remember us promising to come back to help her."

"That may be true in the bright of day, but at night, in the pillow talk between a man and a woman, those promises were made. My mother told me so."

"What else did your mother tell you?"

"As the years passed, her health continued to fade. She had to sell the hotel and we moved to one of the poorer suburbs of Paris. When I was twelve, I worked in a bakery to help keep food on the table. All the time, my mother kept saying how her American friends would come."

Jerome glanced again at the chalice and then asked, “I can understand the confusion, but why did it cause you to start murdering?”

“When I was barely eighteen, my mother died in my arms. In those last hours she realized the folly of her belief any of you would return, and told me the secrets she had kept all of those years.”

“What did she say?”

“My mother told me about you and your men. She told me how you used to visit the hotel and have parties. She told me many of you slept with her. She told me that one of you was my father, but in her shame, she apologized for not being able to tell me who.”

Jerome became defensive and said, “I never slept with your mother, so I cannot be your father.”

“That is what you say now, looking down the barrel of my gun. It could be a convenient lie, but that is not why I sought revenge.”

The Jew looked at the chalice, as did Jean-Claude. Their eyes met and Jerome asked, “Did she tell you about this?”

“Absolutely. My mother told me how you all wanted to chop it up for the money and how she talked you into the tontine. She told me how some of you, in exchange for her silence, promised they would always look after her.”

“Well I wasn't one of them.”

“I know, but unfortunately for you, when you became part of the tontine, you became part of the problem which finds us here today.”

Jerome looked at the gun in his hand and asked, “Did you start killing for revenge or money?”

“It was a little bit of both. My mother died a broken and penniless woman, while the chalice sat silently in a Paris vault. If you had all agreed, the tontine could have been set aside at any time. It was your own personal greed which cost my mother her life. None of you ever called her. None of you ever wrote her. She died and none of you cared."

"So, was it you who left your mother's obituary under my front door? I always wondered who did that and why it was three years old at the time."

"Yes it was I, but I did not slide it under your door. I intentionally dropped it as I was walking out the door."

"What are you saying?"

"My mother knew you had all agreed to stay in touch through you. Since your business has been in the family and at the same place for so long, you were easy to find. I broke into your house one day to find a list of the names and addresses. On my way out, I dropped the newspaper clipping to remind you all of your forgotten promises."

"Why didn't you kill me first?"

"When I found out you were printing the newsletter, I decided you had to be the last one alive. Without someone to come claim the chalice, I could never get it."

"So, it really was the money you were after."

"At first, it might have been, but it was never that simple. I was angry at how you all abandoned my mother. I was angry not knowing which of you was my father. It started out a simple quest to avenge my mother and assuage my honor, but ultimately I began to enjoy killing."

Jerome figured it was best to keep Jean talking, so he asked, "How was it you were able to get away with these murders?"

"The first one, the faggot you called Tinker, was easy. As a pretty young French boy, I had no trouble picking him up at a bar. He took me to his apartment and I killed him."

"What about Sarge?"

"I did regret killing him. In the past, he had come to my mother's aid. The more I thought about it, the angrier I got. If anyone should have honored their promise, he should have. I signed on to work the docks. One night, I sneaked up behind him and used chloroform to knock him out. I laid Sarge on the dock and used the crane to drop the box on him."

"Why didn't you just shoot him or stab him?"

"I was beginning to enjoy what I was doing and I thought making each murder unique would keep the attention of the police. Finding an appropriate murder for each man became my signature."

"Wouldn't you want to avoid the police? Weren't you afraid of being caught?"

"I needed to make sure the news would get back to Paris through the police. The tattoos made the connection between all of you easy, so I made sure the tattoo was plainly visible. The police were looking at individual greed and at each of you. There was no connection to me. I was a stranger to them. As the group got smaller, they never suspected anyone else."

"Fascinating. How did you get to Moocher?"

"Monsieur Carter was easy. Like all of you Americans, he is greedy. I offered to meet him one night to sell him antique jewelry. The irony was, I showed him one of my mother's rings, just before I stuffed him into the safe."

"Who was next?"

"I killed Doctor Fletcher next. Of all the men, I think I hated him the most."

"I saw the photos of your handiwork. Your hatred showed. Why did you hate him so much?"

"The doctor had the least excuse for not looking in on my mother. He came to Europe almost every year to check on the tontine. I saw the records at the bank. Not once in all of that time did he try to contact my mother. For that, I saved something special for him. I arranged to deliver lunch to his office one day. The front door was left unlocked, while all his nurses sat in back and ate their lunch. I pretended to leave by opening and letting the door close. Instead of leaving, I hid in the janitor's closet."

"When everyone left, you came out and killed him. I hate to admit this, but it is fascinating listening to how you did it."

"The next one, Casey, the one you called Cowboy, was far too easy. My mother actually liked him. She called him a little boy in men's clothes. I pretended to be a stable boy. There was so much noise at the rodeo, no one heard me as I whipped him to death."

"Isn't it about the time the FBI got involved?"

"Yes, the agent, what was his name?"

"Sinclair."

"Mon Dieu, how could I forget him. People say we French are obnoxious. He actually helped by deflecting some of the suspicions."

"What do you mean?"

"Every time someone started to suggest another suspect, this FBI man would ignore it. The more others pushed him to explore other possibilities, the more he focused on you."

"That's a fascinating explanation. Go on. Who was killed next?"

"The man in Iowa. The one with the red hair. I appealed to his greed. I stole somebody's farm machine and then told him to meet me to buy a huge insurance policy. He practically jumped in front of the blades himself."

"Fascinating. What about the professor?"

"Killing him was a bit more difficult. The police in Chicago were watching him very tightly. I got a job as a janitor. That gave me the ability to work in the building without raising suspicion. I have learned two important things during my time in America."

"What might those be?"

"You have much too much freedom in this country. Anyone can come and go as they please."

"And what is the other?"

"Everyone runs around so fast. If you have patience and are careful, you can do almost anything without being noticed."

"Interesting. Why did you kill Brownie?"

"I probably regret killing him the most. You can tell by the color of my skin, he was not my father. Unfortunately for him, the only way I could get to the chalice was to kill him. I killed him while two policemen were sitting in the next room."

"How did you do that?"

"I went into the diner and offered to wash dishes in exchange for a meal. Later that night, when he came in to the kitchen, I hit him over the head with a frying pan. Clanging pots and pans don't raise suspicion in a restaurant. The rest of it was simply for style."

"I suppose getting in to kill Carletti wasn't easy."

"Certainly not. He had dozens of guards and that Sinclair fellow was always watching. This was one of those times where my patience paid off. I got hired as a worker and kept a close watch on what went on. Every day I would see this man come and go through the parking garage and the secret door."

"Did you break in or pick the lock on the door?"

"Every night I saw women knock on the secret door in a special way. One night, I showed up a few minutes earlier and knocked the same way. He opened the door expecting to be, how do you say, fucked. I obliged him."

Jerome looked at the cup and then back to Jean-Claude. "I guess that leaves just me?"

Jean smiled and said, "You are correct."

"Do you have some special death planned for me?"

"Why shouldn't I?"

Jerome reasoned, "I never slept with your mother and I never promised to help her, so you have no personal reason to kill me."

"Go on," coaxed Jean-Claude.

"If it's the money you want, we can split the proceeds fifty-fifty."

"Why would I want to do that? I could kill you and keep it all."

"You are right. You could do that, but where would you sell it?"

"What are you offering me?"

"I'm in the jewelry business. If I break it up, discreetly sell the individual gems, and melt down the gold, no one would ever trace it back to you. I could do it for you."

"In exchange for your life?"

"It sounds like a fair trade," offered Jerome.

Jean-Claude thought about it for a minute and then said, "What you say makes sense, but it does deprive me of the pleasure of killing you."

Jean-Claude stood up and walked toward Jerome. He knelt in front of the Jew, still pointing the gun. Jerome was sweating profusely and asked, "What are you doing? I thought we had a deal."

"We do," replied the Frenchman, "but open your mouth first. If I can't kill you, I at least want to hear you beg for your miserable life."

Jerome opened his mouth and Jean-Claude pushed the silencer of the gun between Miller's teeth. Jean-Claude raised his hand, lifting Jerome slightly before telling him, "Okay, Jew. You're going to sell the jewels and give me the money, right?"

From around the barrel, Jerome garbled out, "Yeth. Vat evuh you say."

"Now beg for your life and I'll let you live."

"Pwease don't kill me. Pwease. Pwease wet me wiv."

Jean-Claude relaxed his hand slightly, and then pulled the trigger, blowing bits of Jerome's brain onto the wall. "There now. You see, I can keep promises just as well as you all could."

Jean-Claude picked up Jerome's limp right hand and wrapped it around the grip and trigger of the gun. He held the gun and hand near the Jew's mouth, then let them fall in whatever way gravity decided.

Jean turned and uncorked the bottle of champagne. He poured some into the Calice de Justice and raised it as a toast to Jerome. "I am sorry my friend, but later today someone will find your body. They will find the empty box on the table. They will determine you were despondent over having come so far, only to find your treasure chest empty. Your death will be listed as an unfortunate suicide, while I will be long gone."

Jean-Claude sat down and lifted the cup to his lips, savoring the taste of success and admiring the exquisite craftsmanship which made this moment possible.